Friedrich Hebbel's Conception of Movement in the Absolute and in History

UNC | COLLEGE OF ARTS AND SCIENCES
Germanic and Slavic Languages and Literatures

From 1949 to 2004, UNC Press and the UNC Department of Germanic & Slavic Languages and Literatures published the UNC Studies in the Germanic Languages and Literatures series. Monographs, anthologies, and critical editions in the series covered an array of topics including medieval and modern literature, theater, linguistics, philology, onomastics, and the history of ideas. Through the generous support of the National Endowment for the Humanities and the Andrew W. Mellon Foundation, books in the series have been reissued in new paperback and open access digital editions. For a complete list of books visit www.uncpress.org.

Friedrich Hebbel's Conception of Movement in the Absolute and in History

STEN G. FLYGT

UNC Studies in the Germanic Languages and Literatures
Number 7

Copyright © 1952

This work is licensed under a Creative Commons CC BY-NC-ND license. To view a copy of the license, visit http://creativecommons.org/licenses.

Suggested citation: Flygt, Sten. *Friedrich Hebbel's Conception of Movement in the Absolute and in History.* Chapel Hill: University of North Carolina Press, 1952. DOI: https://doi.org/ 10.5149/9781469657516_Flygt

Library of Congress Cataloging-in-Publication Data
Names: Flygt, Sten G.
Title: Friedrich Hebbel's conception of movement in the absolute and in history / by Sten G. Flygt.
Other titles: University of North Carolina Studies in the Germanic Languages and Literatures ; no. 7.
Description: Chapel Hill : University of North Carolina Press, [1952] Series: University of North Carolina Studies in the Germanic Languages and Literatures. | Includes bibliographical references.
Identifiers: LCCN 53000919 | ISBN 978-1-4696-5750-9 (pbk: alk. paper) | ISBN 978-1-4696-5751-6 (ebook)
Subjects: Hebbel, Friedrich, 1813-1863.
Classification: LCC PD25 .N6 NO. 7

TO

T. MOODY CAMPBELL
Teacher and Friend

PREFACE

The following study was begun in order to find an answer to the question: Do Friedrich Hebbel's plays exhibit a progressive or conservative tendency? As so often happens, the attempt to work out a convincing answer led to the conclusion that the question was incorrectly put, for the notion of a progressive or a static norm of social and historical change turns out to be subordinate, almost incidental, to what I have come to feel is the essential question: What was Hebbel's conception of movement in the Absolute and in history? After the exposition and analysis of the first two parts of this study an attempt is made to answer the re-phrased question. I believe that whatever merit the answer has lies in its suggestiveness and that its defect stems from the limitations of conceptual discourse when used as an instrument of understanding something that lies on a non-conceptual level.

The first part of the study does something that should have been done long ago: it offers a comprehensive discussion of the passages in the diaries and letters, with some reference to the poems, which express or reflect Hebbel's thoughts about social and historical progress. It has, of course, been pointed out that Hebbel was not consistent in his views of this question, but there has been a strong tendency, especially on the part of those students of Hebbel who find in all his plays a turning point which marks the beginning of a higher type of society, to ignore the inconsistency and overlook its significance. In the following pages the inconsistency is shown to be fundamental and persistent, revealing itself in an oscillation between periods of "progressivism" and periods of "conservatism" in Hebbel's life.

The second section is given over to a discussion of the dramas apart from the diaries and letters, partially in order not to dilute the evidence which is collected and presented in the first part, and partially to disclose more deftly the threads of internal relationship passing from play to play. The analysis of the plays, of course, cannot pretend to be completely new and different. Indeed, such a pretense would challenge disbelief. But the analysis does show that there exists in Hebbel's dramatic production the same kind of oscillation as was established for the diaries and letters, and it is believed that Parts One and Two of the study, when taken together, will make quite clear the inadequacy of any

PREFACE

"Wendepunkt-Theorie." The third part then ventures to suggest that it is not the direction but the nature of the movement in the Absolute and in history which is the basic question for Hebbel. It is hoped that the analyses and conclusions of the present study will make some positive contribution to the discussion of what is still a rather controversial issue in Hebbel-scholarship.

S.G.F.

Middletown, Conn.
February 6, 1952

PART ONE

Discursive Formulations: The Diaries and Letters

PART ONE

DISCURSIVE FORMULATIONS: THE DIARIES
AND LETTERS

". . . und wenn man den Shakespeare einmal zum Zeugen für die Nichtigkeit des Lebens aufruft und nicht hinzufügt, dass er an einem andern Ort mit gleichem Ernst von dem hohen und einzigen Wert des Lebens redet, so sündigt man gegen ihn . . . ." Hebbel, Tagebücher, 19.Dez.1843.

It becomes abundantly clear after only a superficial consideration that Hebbel's universe is in constant flux; *Panta rhei* is for him a fixed principle that governs the mystic processes of the cosmos as well as the struggle of nations and men. This much can be said with certainty at the outset.

It is not at all certain, however, that Hebbel can with justice be made out a champion of social progress, a Hegelian who conceived of the death of an Agnes Bernauer as helping by a process of metaphysical dialectic to make a class intermarriage possible for members of subsequent generations.[1]

In fact, as has been noted,[2] there seems to have been a great deal of inconsistency in Hebbel's beliefs about whether or not life progresses because of the conflict between the individual and the Absolute. Indeed, painstaking examination of Hebbel's diaries, letters and poems will not only reveal inconsistency in this regard, but shows that there was in Hebbel's feeling and thinking on this point a kind of alternation between periods of time in which he tended to be progressive and others in which he tended to be conservative. And it is possible even to make a correlation, though necessarily a rather vague one because of the lag which is natural between a spiritual reorientation and its expression in a major work, between a generally progressive or generally conservative mental set as revealed in poems, letters, and diaries, and the various plays.

Although the idea of progress is frequently taken to mean change for the better in the status or condition of a social group, it does not require much reflection to realize that a consideration of the progress of an individual is a more simple and perhaps even primary aspect of the whole question. Thus in our study of progressivism and conservatism in Friedrich Hebbel it will be necessary to examine how he regarded the universal process of change and flux as affecting not only a state, a social class, but also a single human being.

When, therefore, the poems, letters, diaries, are examined with a view toward learning how Hebbel expressed his thoughts and feelings about the question of change and flux, whether for society or for the individual, it is revealed that in his earliest period, as is natural at an age of extreme youth, he was inclined to a rather naive faith in progress. This early phase of naive progressivism runs to about the end of 1838, but, of course, it must be borne in mind that for a matter as gradual as a shift in general outlook it is not appropriate to attempt to fix any kind of clear cut *terminus* either *ante quem* or *post quem*.

The earliest significant utterance would seem to be four lines of verse[3] from his eighteenth year to the effect that many a transformation is not necessarily a metamorphosis into a higher form, as of caterpillar into butterfly, but that the opposite change, of butterfly into caterpillar, also takes place. Thus the key-note of ambivalence is struck at the outset and the problematic antithesis is stated at once. Two years later in a rather long rhymed reflection[4] on his relation to nature, he expresses the feeling of a vital human nisus towards the godhead. And it is much the same feeling that is expressed in a poem called "Rosenleben,"[5] an impetuous urge to advance to highest perfection, but it is tempered by the solemn realization that the individual must perish. And even in this earliest stage a note of conservatism is struck in a verse plea to spare an old house for reason of sentiment.[6]

Conservative sentiment, however, is overshadowed by defiant egotism. It is against a background of penury, disillusionment with friends and benefactors in Hamburg and a desperate struggle to acquire skill and information so readily mastered by his fellow students in Heidelberg and Munich, none of whom could match him in decisiveness, maturity, and penetration, that a letter to Elise Lensing[7] must be read. He tells her that if she has the feeling that he is somewhat set apart and above others, she should also realize that in a difference between himself and the world he may be right even though the world is at least not wrong. To be sure, *Welt* in this passage is probably not to be taken in too metaphysical a sense, none the less it is interesting to note the passage as an expression of Hebbel's feeling, however transient, that the individual may be justified in opposing society: a progressive and perhaps revolutionary point of view. An even more naive progressivism is expressed in a letter to Emil Rousseau,[8] in which he assigns to the poet the task of illuminating the critical relations of the individual and the Absolute or, to anticipate his later terminology, Idea. In this connection he believes that he can detect progress in the great representatives of literature, Dante being more comprehensive than Homer, Goethe more translucent than Shakespeare. The same kind of naive progressivism is expressed in another letter to Rousseau,[9] in which he speaks of a feeling of revulsion that everything, no matter how splendid, must give way to something still more splendid. In a different mood, however, he goes so far as to see a proof for the existence of God in the upward movement of nature towards a culmination: since man feels that he is not this culmination, it must exist outside him in a higher being, or God.[10]

Until the end of the year 1838 Hebbel's reflections on progress continue in this same vein: the best thing about religion is that it produces heretics;[11] the individual will not die as long as he possesses the capacity for growth;[12] the principle of evil is unstable, changing ultimately into good;[13] one should never give up the resolution to change, even after change has become impossible.[14] On the twenty-eighth of November, however, he made an entry in his diary which two years later he was to call the most profound observation in the whole book,[15] that man is the continuance of the act of creation, which prevents the world from coming to a halt, growing rigid and petrified. In the present context this observation seems to fit in with the generally progressive outlook that has been apparent thus far, but it is significant that on the same day there is another entry[16] in the diaries to the effect that it is scarcely a comfort that we are constantly ascending, since we will always remain on the ladder. This observation rather modifies the force of the one immediately preceding, which is, indeed, one of the most profound entries in all the diaries, half revealing, half concealing Hebbel's primal poetic-religious experience.

The strain of conservatism which was glimpsed in the early verses is present also in the diaries and letters, less prominent at first than the progressive strain but attaining very definite expression in November, 1838, shortly after the death of his mother and of his dearest friend, Emil Rousseau. Its earliest expression in the diaries comes in 1835,[17] as the tragic or perhaps cynical feeling that it is the lot of the unusual individual to be destroyed: it is an old story that flints must be broken to pieces if they are to give off sparks. This, too, is a revealing statement, which hints at Hebbel's concept of tragic experience for the individual, his mystic belief that individuation is a sin against the Absolute which must be expiated by re-absorption of the individual into the Whole. It is a belief which obviously cannot be called progressive and optimistic as far as the individual is concerned, and yet cannot be put on the conservative side because it may be interpreted, and those critics who take Hebbel's basic position to involve a belief in social progress do so interpret it, as meaning that the individual must perish in order that society or humanity may advance. Since this is in a sense the crux of the problem of progressivism and conservatism in Hebbel, this, and all similar expressions of belief in the tragic insignificance of the individual in relation to the Idea, must be put down in a class by themselves. Moreover, what is true for the individual may also be true for the human race: the world is a unique residue after God's self-purification, the constantly collapsing bridge from nature to God, the end of the convulsive struggle is exhaustion and the only hope is for the total extinction of life;[18] the individual stands in the same relationship to nature as a variation to a musical theme, and God can enjoy a blissful self-subsistence without humanity to be nurtured and cared for.[19] Thus man, both collectively and individually, is of no moment to the Deity, though he may be used by the Deity for the attainment of some great purpose, by being flung beneath the wheels, to impede for a moment, or change, the course of the great cosmic juggernaut. A tragedy based on the story of Jeanne d'Arc would thus have to produce the impression of affording a glimpse into the eternal order of nature which not even the Deity can disturb with impunity.[20] A purpose for which it is conceivable that the Deity would disturb the eternal order of nature would be the elevation of humanity, but the masses make no progress, we read elsewhere in the diaries.[21] And a bit later the doubts about the possibility of progress find such expressions as these: Mankind holds on to every error that might help it; it would believe in immortality even though having knowledge of the contrary; it could be that the higher life produces nothing more than a cozy web of useful illusions, though that would, to be sure, be so extraordinary that a creature capable of having such wise and divine dreams, might deserve and even effect their realization.[22] Germination and corruption are not far removed from each other and usually identical.[23]

There now ensues a long period in Hebbel's development in which neither a progressive nor a conservátive outlook seems to predominate. It is a period of sharp and irregular fluctuation between the two points of view. It runs roughly from the end of 1838, when he faced the necessity of soon leaving Munich for Hamburg, to approximately the fall of 1846 after his marriage to Christine Enghaus. It is the period in which *Judith, Genoveva, Der Diamant,* and *Maria Magdalene* were written, *Moloch* and *Julia* begun. It is a second period of expansion and emergence from the narrow circle of Hamburg to which he returned on foot in the late winter of 1839 and where he was tormented by his equivocal relationship with Elise Lensing. It was an emergence made possible by the travel stipend granted him early in 1842 by Christian VIII of Denmark which took him to Paris, Rome, Naples, and Vienna, and brought him into contact with people of social, intellectual, and artistic distinction. The period culminates in a rather decided turn towards progressivism.[24]

Let us survey first the utterances from the diaries, letters, and poems of this period which are concerned primarily with the process of change or flux and then, as before, consider those which are concerned with the helpless plight of man in opposition to the Absolute or are unequivocally conservative.

It now becomes more apparent than before that although Hebbel was convinced of the actuality of change and flux in the universe and in society, he was by no means convinced that the process of change was in the direction of some better condition, either for mankind or the individual. The process of change might be merely a re-formation of the same substance: the sun shines bright; it melts the icicles along the roof, they drip down merrily in order to turn into ice again below.[25] On the other hand, he can also write of the possibility of change for the better in the individual, it being the province of art to show this life process, by which man's inmost being evolves, the good evoking the bad and this in turn the better, and so on without limit.[26] A little more than a year later, after the completion of *Judith*, he writes in a letter to the actress Auguste Stich-Crelinger, which, as he frequently did, he incorporated in the diaries,[27] that *Judith* is based upon a conception that in extraordinary crises of world history the Deity intervenes directly in the course of events and causes monstrous deeds to be done by people who would certainly do no such thing of their own volition. This was the case with Judith, who was compelled to murder Holofernes when he was about to destroy the Chosen People from whom salvation was to come. Other entries in the diaries for the same month agree with this progressive, teleological concept of history. He wonders whether the chronicle of great attainments is good for mankind, which must be paralyzed by the awareness of unsurpassable greatness, and so, if the vital spring of creativity is not to be choked by the accumulations of the past, Shakespeare, Goethe, all giants must be swept away, a terrible and insupportable thought.[28] Life is an unceasing process of becoming; to regard oneself as having come to the end of this process is to put an end to one's life.[29] A little later, however, he regards the life process very differently: Neither fixity nor progress, only movement is the purpose of life,[30] a direct contradiction of the evolutionary concept of history which he embodied in *Judith* and which was supported by his study of Jeanne d'Arc, whom he seems to have regarded as a parallel to Judith: God had to perform a miracle to maintain the independence of France, because it was from France that the revolution was to proceed.[31] But whether or not progress takes place, whether there is revolution or evolution, the highest law of life for both states and individuals is the law of self-maintenance. If the old form has strength enough to resist the new, then it is certain that the new form does not yet have strength enough to unite all the elements which must be united after the destruction of the old.[32] The law of self-maintenance operates with brutal disregard of personal feelings and morality; it visits murder and torment upon the free rebellious spirits whom its own repressive laws have called into being. So runs a sonnet[33] dated the third of September 1841. Yet, we are told in another sonnet[34] dated only two days later, the history of the world tries to fashion out of fragile material a pure image of humanity, which we can glimpse only when the shrouding mist is lifted momentarily; in our limited vision we reverence the mere fragments which are chipped off the block from which the image is being fashioned, and which can ultimately be completed; then in the presence of its perfect totality the imperfect individual will pass away. A third sonnet[35] written at the same time recommends that the poet, whose task it is to mirror the struggle between old and new, have reverence for the forms of life which emerge too late. This admonition is very interesting, inasmuch as it was Hebbel's view that all poetry is dramatic, that is, progressively productive, and that an idea which does not generate a series of new ideas is unpoetic, for life is revealed only in the form of transition.[36] Indeed transition is the highest law of life,[37] which can exist only through a pendulum-like alternation between poles. And the most beautiful symbol of life is the fly which perishes in copulation: all its existence is only a preparation for the highest moment which is also the moment of dissolution, in which the spark is transmitted to a new being—an endless chain which always leads to the climax and never beyond it.[38]

Eighteen forty-three, the year of *Maria Magdalene,* is a year in which the pertinent diary entries revolve about the nature of vital and historical change. As we have seen above, the highest law of life is transition, but it is at least possible that life can be manifested only in a rising and falling line, that sin is a necessary consequence of goodness, because goodness cannot be maintained at a peak and cannot go beyond it and so on.[39] In a letter to Eduard Duller he takes a more positive view, saying that Duller, like himself, has been compelled to descend into regions where ordinary eyes perceive only the terror of decay and not the germs of new life.[40] Then the notion of the pendulum-movement of history recurs: all movement in history is a gradual transition from one extreme to another and back rather than a reconciliation of extremes.[41] In literature, specifically the drama, he hopes to see real progress: Shakespeare must be surpassed by a new form of the drama in which not merely the critical relation of the individual to the Idea, but the justification of the Idea itself is to be debated.[42] This passage, of course, is related to the problem which he posed in *Maria Magdalene,* about which he wrote to Elise Lensing:[43] all the characters are justified and yet the collision of these opposing natures sets a terrible destiny into motion; in the background are ideas of family, morality, and honor which will be universally accepted possibly only after centuries. The collision of opposing natures in a way mirrors the pendulum-movement of history: the poet will express his ideas dialectically in the same way that the world and life are dialectic and every phenomenon evokes its opposite.[44]

As has already been noted on p. 3 above, on the twenty-eighth of November 1838, Hebbel made an entry in his diaries which two years later he called the most profound observation in the entire book: the existence of man brings life and movement into the world, which would otherwise be rigid. The logical consequence of this is that the necessary condition for historical or social change, whether this change be progressive or merely oscillatory, is a conflict between the eternal rigidity of the Absolute and the transient mobility of the individual. Hebbel was quite right in his judgment that the observation cited was the most profound in his entire book. Some notion of the full significance, it is hoped, will be revealed by the present study, especially the concluding section. Special mention is made of it here because in the spring of 1844 Hebbel made two significant and related entries in his diary:

> What is rationally good for the individual may be the most irrational thing for the universe. What could be more rational for the individual than to wish for eternal youth, in which all his powers of development and effectiveness are at their maximum? And yet what is more irrational for the universe?[45]

Thus the first entry. The second makes it clear why this must be so:

> At the moment when the elixir of eternal life is discovered, human beings will no longer be able to reproduce themselves—the well-spring will run dry. There will be no further death, but also no further birth.[46]

Thus it is apparent that the individual must be sacrificed in order that the Absolute may live and move.

From this point in Hebbel's development until the end of the period we are now considering he fluctuates very strongly, almost rhythmically, between an evolutionary and a pessimistic view of cosmic and historical change. The evolutionary or optimistic view finds such expression as the elegiac couplets entitled "Verschiedener Casus"[47] which proclaim (ironically to modern ears) that there need be no fear that the Russians will conquer Germany as the Germans conquered Rome, until the Russians have improved upon *Tasso* or the Germans upon the knout, or those entitled "Jetziger Standpunkt der Geschichte:"[48] "What has history achieved so far? The eternal ideas! Now the task of history is to realize them." Or, again, he speaks[49] of the process of refinement as the highest principle of nature both in the physical and mental realm: from rock to plant, from plant to animal, from animal to man, and in man to genius. In sharp contrast is this pessimistic view of change: "Death! The constant succession of generations on the same level, the last being no more than the first!"[50] Yet he feels that even though it is a serious error on Hegel's part to suppose that art can be surpassed, there can be an ultimate and supreme stage of art.[51] Then the idea recurs that life and movement are purchased only by the sacrifice of the individual: No human being can be born unless another dies just before.[52] And thus, more than a year later, an interesting side light on his conception of production and change in nature:[53] It is very probable that nature must create everything that it can create, but also that a crisis will occur, as soon as nature might be able to do no more than repeat itself in order not to stop producing. Then he adds: "I am *almost* convinced of this." The creation of life he conceives of as occurring at the point where all limits cross and all contradictions touch each other.[54]

The process of constant and violent fluctuation we have just touched in the period under consideration seems to have come to an at least temporary halt with the attainment of an optimistic view. On the sixth of October 1846, he recorded in his diary[55] that he is firmly convinced that some day the world will attain a form corresponding to what the noblest members of the human race think and feel; however, even then, bestial and diabolical creatures will not vanish but will only be bound.

So much for the utterances which are concerned primarily with change and progress in this period of fluctuation. The impression gained from them is strengthened if we briefly consider also the utterances from the same period which deal with the hopeless plight of the individual or have an outright conservative tendency.

Most of Hebbel's speculations about the relation of the individual to the Absolute are pessimistic as regards the individual, that is, for the individual the cosmic process ends in defeat, usually even without the consolation of being ennobled or elevated in any way, and it is only the nonentity who can escape this tragic fate.[56] Sometimes, however, Hebbel does seem to have at least the hope that the individual will reach a higher form through the tragic experience.[57] But usually he feels that, even though the individual may be dedicated to the service of a divine purpose, as represented in *Judith*, none the less the individual is necessarily sinful by virtue of being an individual and thus cannot avoid tragedy.[58] All life is a struggle of the individual with the Absolute.[59] It is a struggle which an individual of any dimensions cannot escape and in which sin against the Absolute is implicit. In a passage which is very important for his conception of tragic guilt, Hebbel writes: God will not attach decisive significance to the sins of sinful individuals against each other but only to the sins against the Idea itself, and there actual and only possible sins are completely identical.[60] Man's freedom of will consists merely in his freedom to acquiesce to the inevitable.[61] The evidence is thus for the most part clearly against the supposition that Hebbel believed in the possibility of progress for the individual during this period.

If we now search for utterances during the same period which are conservative in their tendency, that is, show a static conception of history, or the conception that historical change is merely an oscillation between extremes, or express the view that progress is illusory, or that it may even be desirable to resist change, it is possible to find a good many in addition to the ones already mentioned in connection with the discussion of the fluctuation in Hebbel's conception of historical change or transition.

Attention has been called, on p. 3, to the very significant idea that the individual is the principle of mobility in the Absolute, which but for this would be lifeless and rigid. This idea is to be connected with the diary entry of the twenty-fourth of February 1839[62] to the effect that there can be nothing completely new in the world, nothing which has not already been in existence: it is only that an element disappears at one place and reappears at another. The disappearance and reappearance of the elements must under this view constitute historical change, which a progressivist or surely a revolutionary would not only welcome but even assist. A thoroughly consistent progressivist would not say, as Hebbel does in one place:[63] "Whoever directs humanity back within its boundaries, does a much more meritorious deed than one who supports it in its striving towards the infinite." Indeed, the striving of mankind towards the infinite may be a completely illusory idea and Herder's notion of the perfectibility of humanity is contrary to history and also unreasonable, because the human race consists of transient individuals, who would endure great injustice if the twelfth millennium realized things which the sixth had rejected as mere dreams.[64]

The other entries and observations which belong in the present category add nothing new or significant to what we already know: the cosmic process is symbolized in the two buckets in a well;[65] the world is a constantly renewed digestive tract through which the same old material passes;[66] the constant repetition of the same things must produce a sense of disgust with life;[67] history is merely an oscillating movement;[68] everything *is* from the beginning—nothing becomes, it merely changes form.[69] It can all be summed up by the diary entry from October 1844 (p. 9) to the effect that the generations of mankind merely succeed but never surpass each other.

In the fall of 1846, as will be recalled, Hebbel seems to have arrived at a much more optimistic view, an attitude of political progressivism, which seems to have predominated in his outlook until the spring, roughly March, of 1848 when it was succeeded by another short period during which progressivism and conservatism were approximately equally balanced. The period of progressivism, coming shortly after his marriage to Christine Enghaus, is the period of *Ein Trauerspiel in Sizilien,* of the completion of *Julia,* and the beginning of *Herodes und Mariamne,* which was completed during the subsequent transition to the final period of conservatism. The period of political progressivism which we are about to discuss was a period of political unrest in Europe culminating in the democratic revolutionary movements of 1848, which, it may be noted here, had a sobering rather than exhilarating effect on Hebbel.

The reasons why it is possible, though perhaps a bit incautious, to speak of a period of political progressivism between the latter part of 1846 and the early part of 1848 is that, beginning with the diary entry of the sixth of October 1846, which, as we have already noted, speaks of Hebbel's firm conviction that mankind is making progress towards a social paradise, most of the few expressions bearing on the subject express the same attitude. He writes in his diary on the eighth of January 1847[70] that he explained to Prechtler, though actually for his own benefit, that

the problem of conflict between the existing form of the state
and the significant individual who has progressed beyond the
state is to be solved by the growing realization on the part of the
individual of a higher form of the state. Still, at another time in
the same month[71] he speaks of the tragic hero, i.e., the individual,
as being in the same relation to the Idea as a disease is to the organism. And at still another time[72] he writes of his doubts about
the possibility of there being a history of the human race at all,
in the sense that it would be possible to speak of an advance of the
Weltgeist in knowledge of itself; these are doubts which, to be
sure, are not for daily use, but as a remedy for a surfeit of Herder-
Hegelian constructs of the so-called world historical process. It is
interesting that these skeptical reservations are written as though
they were really no more than just that, and as if his basic convictions are actually in agreement with Herder's and Hegel's
optimistic idealism. In accordance with this, his first comments
upon the revolutionary movements of 1848 are affirmative, even
enthusiastic. To Ludwig Gurlitt he writes:[73] "What do you say
about France? For Germany and all Europe I expect the most
salutary results from this event which has happened with such
surprising rapidity. But it is easy to prophesy, since the results
are already becoming manifest everywhere!" Indeed, this enthusiasm went so far as to cause him to project a play about an
appropriate political subject, *Das erste Todesurteil*. As we learn
from his diary[74] the impulse for the play came from a sense of exhilaration at living in a new Austria in which he felt more secure
than Prince Metternich, in which there were to be freedom of the
press, national armament, and a constitution. This drama, which
he conceived immediately after reading the emperor's last proclamation, was to have the following outline: a monarch is convinced by a serious miscarriage of justice caused by his minister
not only of his own inadequacy as an absolute ruler, but also of
human inadequacy in general, and determines to institute constitutional government, freedom of the press, and so on. Hebbel's enthusiasm was not long unqualified. Only ten days later[75]
he was much sobered by the attempt at bloody repression of the
demonstrations in Berlin: he was oppressed by the thought of the
suffering that confronted his own time and could rejoice only
when he thought of future generations. His misgivings continued
to increase even though the new political liberalization brought

him personal gains: his dramas could now be performed in the Hofburgtheater in Vienna. Still, he did not feel he was enough of a child to be happy about this turn of events: he didn't like the taste of the egg that had been roasted in the world conflagration.[76]

His misgivings grew as time went on, but for a while, until about the middle of 1851, they seem to have been approximately balanced by continued hope and belief in political progress. The misgivings seem to have stemmed both from a growing insight into the brutality of revolutionary movements and from a disillusionment: war is the liberty of certain barbarians, therefore, it is no wonder that they love it;[77] communism can triumph momentarily, that is, can maintain itself until it has revealed all its terrors and saturated humanity with loathing that will be sufficient for all time;[78] half a victory of the idea is worse than a total defeat.[79] Still, both for the individual and for a whole nation, there may come a moment of time in which it can sit in judgment upon itself, when it has the occasion to repair the past and cast off old sins. At such times, Nemesis will be standing by, however, and woe to both nation and individual if it takes the wrong road. This, of course, is the situation of Herodes, in *Herodes und Mariamne*, but it is also the situation of Germany in 1848.[80] Hebbel continues to hope that the revolutionary movements actually will repair the past and at times thinks he sees signs that the social conflicts which he illuminated in his dramas are being debated in the streets and reaching an actual solution, so that his drama will no longer have to concern itself with negative criticisms of crumbling social conditions.[81] *Maria Magdalene*, of course, was the drama which was concerned directly with criticism of contemporary social conditions. Now he expresses the hope that *Julia*, the, so to speak, second and positive half of *Maria Magdalene*, will be more apposite to the times.[82]

The hope that the revolutionary movements would actually repair the past was one that he expressed more confidently to others than to himself. Indeed, if violent fluctuation of attitude toward the question of social progress were not the rule in Hebbel, as we have seen it is, it would be very hard to believe that within four days of his writing to Gustav Kühne in an optimistic vein about the positive solution of social conflict, he should enter in his diary an observation of profound conservatism.[83] It is, in fact, a statement of the idea, which, changed very slightly in the outward aspect of the metaphor, illuminates the significance of *Gyges und sein Ring* in Kandaules' famous speech about the sleep of the world. In his diary Hebbel writes:

> They are now tearing up the paving of the state and society. I have a strange feeling about it. I feel as though the structure which is being destroyed now were built upon primal experiences made under conditions such as are becoming actual again, as though every paving block bore on its reverse side the inscription: We too know that this is a paving block, even though we have carved the image of a god upon it; it will be your task to see how you will get along without paving blocks that people take to be more than paving blocks!

In Kandaules' speech, of course, the essentially worthless objects which have a right to veneration are the veil, the crown, and the sword, which Kandaules had felt blocked the road to progress, but which, as he came to understand, are a source of strength to mankind.

On the last day of December 1848, looking back over the eventful and turbulent year, the political changes which it had wrought and in which he had taken some part as a member of a delegation which had besought the emperor to return to Vienna from Innsbruck as a necessary step toward the restoration of peace and quiet, Hebbel wrote in his diary:[84] "We will probably never succeed in erecting an imposing and well-based political structure. Still, it seems that absolutism has been swept aside and, I should hope, cannot return. And that, alone, is an immeasurable gain." From a letter to Gustav Kühne written probably in 1849,[85] we learn that the well-based and imposing political structure that Hebbel would like to see can and should be only a rational expansion of the old structure and that the foundations of society should not be torn up. But this essentially conservative outlook is balanced by expressions of a decidedly anti-conservative point of view: the illnesses which signify the course of humanity are called revolutions;[86] a real conservative may not even wash himself;[87] it is a great error to suppose that the earth can return to the old center of gravity which it has lost, as though it would ever have lost it, if there had been enough pull in it to paralyze the elements which were pushing ahead.[88] Thus, the optimistic progressivism we have seen is abruptly checked by the political events of 1848, regains some force for a time and then subsides more and more as the conservative strain comes to the fore. Into this emergent phase of the final conservative period fall Hebbel's comedy, *Der Rubin*, and the completion of the second act of *Moloch*.

The next significant expression from the diaries and letters bearing upon the problem of progressivism and conservatism was written on the fourteenth of September 1851[89] and it is conservative in tone: No matter what one may believe about the relationship of the new era to the old, it is certain that the new era has been living on mere concepts, whereas the old era had an immeasurable and, to be sure, mystic background of ideas, as can be seen in the contrast of Catholicism and Protestantism, absolutism and constitutionalism. The *Nachspiel zur Genoveva* was completed on the twenty-first of January 1851. The work of writing *Agnes Bernauer* had begun on the twenty-second of September.[90] It was completed on the twenty-fourth of December in the same year. Some time after the first of the year 1851, then, can be considered as the beginning of the last period in the history of Hebbel's orientation towards progressivism and conservatism. Its general tendency towards conservatism received an impetus from a disillusioned reaction to revolutionary excesses and was subject to certain deviations in the direction of progressivism, as must now, in view of the development of Hebbel's views up to this time, be considered inevitable. It is the period not only of the *Nachspiel zur Genoveva* and *Agnes Bernauer*, but also of *Gyges und sein Ring*, of *Die Nibelungen*, and of the unfinished *Demetrius*. It is the period in which Hebbel's fame was assured, in which he enjoyed the little domestic happiness that was granted him, in which he acquired a home of his own, moved in the highest social circles of Germany, received public honors. The sense of tradition, which had never been absent in Hebbel (he was well versed in the history of Schleswig-Holstein and pride in the deeds of his ancestral Dithmarschen was a strong component of his boyhood fantasy, finding such concrete expression as his poem, "Die Schlacht bei Hemmingstedt," published in 1833), came to the fore again, and with it the shift of interest in the story of Agnes Bernauer from the tragedy of beauty to the tragedy of politico-metaphysical necessity. From this time on, Hebbel referred quite often to his *Agnes Bernauer* as evidence that he was not revolutionary in his political tendencies. He felt that he had never before so clearly perceived the relationship between the individual and the state and that surely the criticism could not be made of this play that it attacked social conventions and order.[91] It does, he feels, demonstrate that the individual, no matter how splendid, great, beautiful, or noble it may be, must under all circumstances, submit to society because, in society and in its necessary formal expression, the state, all mankind is embodied, but in the individual only a single aspect of humanity is revealed. This, he maintains, is the basic position of all his plays.[92]

As Hebbel looked back, in December 1851, over the year just ended, he thought that the world situation had gained some stability and that a period was about to begin in which the opposing forces could, on the basis of the experiences they had had, work toward a lasting reconciliation. This was his pious wish for the future.[93] He was, therefore, profoundly shocked at the performance of a play called *Otto von Wittelsbach* when someone called out Da capo! after the scene in which the emperor was assassinated. Such brutality and stupidity he considered the most shocking thing he had ever heard, ample justification, not only for strict censorship, but even for closing the theaters.[94] Hebbel seems now convinced of the fact that, as his *Agnes Bernauer* teaches, respect is due to the eternal institutions of the world,[95] and even when he professes to be convinced that the world will fight its way through to purer and higher forms, he declares that the unfolding of the entire man, which is the goal of social progress, must be based upon reverence.[96] The capacity to feel this kind of reverence for representatives of the collective forces (e.g., the state) he feels has been to a large degree lost by the people of his time, so that even the wife of a prominent diplomat in Vienna was not able to sympathize with the last scene of *Agnes Bernauer*, even though Duke Ernst is without any question the fully justified representative of the collective forces.[97] An attempt on the life of the emperor evokes in him, together with gratitude for the fact that it was unsuccessful, a sense of shocked indignation, since an unsuccessful attempt of this sort is worse than any other actual crime, hitting, as it does, at every individual through the representative of all. The fact that this view is not universally acknowledged he connects with the circumstance that a play like *Agnes Bernauer* can be rejected.[98] Hebbel seems to have no doubt whatever that the state in a situation such as he portrayed in *Agnes Bernauer* has the right to demand the sacrifice of an individual life, no matter how innocent.[99] He insists upon the fact that he is entirely on the side of Duke Ernst and maintains that it was the character of the duke that originally interested him in the subject (an assertion that we may well doubt in view of the evidence for Hebbel's early concern with the tragedy of beauty which has been presented by R. M. Werner, Meyer-Benfey and others). The necessity of putting Agnes to death, he says, springs from the fact that the rights of the individual count for nothing in a situation which endangers the foundations on which they rest.[100]

From the passage just cited it can be seen that at least at the beginning of the last period of his life, the time during which he wrote both *Agnes Bernauer* and *Gyges und sein Ring*, his outlook was almost unequivocally conservative, for there is practically nothing from this period to redress the balance unless it is a brief passage from a letter to Adolph Pichler[101] to the effect that the disease of self-destruction which has attacked the world is, after all, only the wholesome consequence of unhealthy conditions. By 1856, however, after he had begun work on *Die Nibelungen*, there is some relaxation of this uncomprising conservatism and again we read in the diaries[102] that the Absolute is indeed eternal but manifests itself only in transient phenomena, whose will to overprolong their existence constitutes the tragic curse. The transient phenomenal manifestations of the Absolute which outlive themselves, are, of course, not only individuals, but also social institutions. Ethical forces, Christianity, for example, which are manifest only in times of great change, are corrupted and perverted soon after their victory. This is a circumstance which Hebbel says he has always taken to prove that progress is possible only for the individual.[103] This observation seems to take us back to his earlier remarks that the process of historical change consists only in an alternation of outward forms. The barbarian who destroys the forms of the civilization he attacks, the books and other works of art of that civilization, will necessarily have to re-create those forms, if only after centuries.[104]

The interest in the ebb and flow of history, in the alternation of forms, which comes to the fore again and modifies the very nearly reactionary outlook we have noted, Hebbel himself interprets conservatively. Contrasting himself with certain other men of letters, he writes to Uechtritz[105] that the bizarre and violent aspects of his plays are due to the fact that he is concerned with the self-correction and revision of the world, the sudden and unforeseen delivery of the moral principle. In fact, Hebbel seems to fancy himself as a very moral writer and professes in a letter to Georg Cotta,[106] which is written at least partly for effect, that to call him anything but unpretentious and conservative is a crude distortion of truth. The rather ironical tone of the letter, however, does not alter the fact that he was probably in earnest about calling Cotta's attention to the fact that the four plays which he had written since 1848 were anything but revolutionary: *Herodes und Mariamne* represents Christianity as the most elevated instrument of culture, *Michel Angelo* teaches deep humility, *Agnes Bernauer* shows the state to be the basic condition of all human prosperity which may demand any sacrifice, and *Gyges und sein Ring* celebrates the eternal rights of custom and tradition.

There are only a few more passages to be cited on the progressive side of the account which we have been making of Hebbel's attitude toward the question of progressivism and conservatism, and these passages are not very progressive in tone. We read that the belief in God and immortality is the only thing which has made society and progress possible;[107] that all progress which the world has made has come about through great individuals who were a law unto themselves and broke with the established views and conditions; individuals are shadows of the species and, like them, fade away.[108] Two diary entries, however, which belong under the general heading of change or flux must be emphasized in passing. They are variations of a feeling or belief that we have encountered before in substantially the same form. The earlier one reads: "You breathe in another's death as your life and another's life out as your death."[109] The latter one, one of the last entries made, reads:

> If it ever should come to depend upon the will of any generation of the human race, whether it wished to live forever, but under the condition that no one else be either born or resurrected from the dead, might perhaps some minority, who would feel regret for the sake of Caesar and Alexander, Shakespeare and Goethe, Phidias and Raphael, and who would not wish to forfeit the geniuses of the future, reject this possibility, and could it accomplish anything?[110]

The remaining passages to be entered on the conservative side of the ledger are also quickly summed up: In art, as in everything that is alive, there is no progress, only different kinds of stimulus.[111] Since Hebbel rejects Herder's belief in the infinite perfectibility of the race and instead holds that nature reaches a high point only in the individual, he is not fanatical about the monarchical or republican form of government.[112] Christianity is one of several mythologies and not necessarily the most profound.[113]

Hebbel's view of the individual, as the helpless pawn of vast forces, however, has not grown less poignant. It is his conclusion that where great catastrophes have come about, they have resulted not from the short-sightedness or wickedness of the persons playing a prominent role in history but through the action of some law.[114] History is a mill in which the living believe they are toiling but in which phantoms perform the work.[115] He cannot take a calm and dispassionate view of the cosmic tragic process, knows no consolation for the loss of the individual, even though it may only be a pet squirrel.[116] The individual is doomed merely by virtue of being an individual, the passive perfect beauty of an Agnes Bernauer can set off a tragic and deadly conflict.[117] The helplessness of the individual comes from the fact that it is his particular existence which brings movement into the Absolute, is the necessary pre-condition of the cosmic process. As we have seen, Hebbel's views about the direction of the cosmic process are self-contradictory and fluctuate in small oscillations and large rhythmic movements embracing the oscillations much as a billow embraces wavelets. From first to last, however, he is consistent in his belief that the Absolute is prevented from growing rigid only by the stream of individuals: there is no remedy for death and there can be none because nature has made the total life process dependent upon the, so to speak, metabolic flow of individuals, just as the individual life process is dependent upon the metabolic flow of basic substances.[118]

PART TWO
Dramatic Formulations: The Plays

PART TWO

DRAMATIC FORMULATIONS: THE PLAYS

"Der Dualismus geht durch alle unsre Anschauungen und Gedanken, durch jedes einzelne Moment unsres Seins hindurch, und er selbst ist unsre höchste, letzte Idee. Wir haben ganz und gar ausser ihm keine Grund-Idee. Leben und Tod, Krankheit und Gesundheit, Zeit und Ewigkeit, wie Eins sich gegen das Andere abschattet, können wir uns denken und vorstellen, aber nicht das, was als Gemeinsames, Lösendes und Versöhnendes hinter diesen gespaltenen Zweiheiten liegt." Hebbel, Tagebücher, 2.Dez.1840.

For Hebbel art was not only infinitely more than a projection of the world of phenomena, it was also something quite different, namely philosophy made actual, just as the world is the Idea (i.e. God or the Absolute) made actual.[1] For him any philosophy which did not culminate and manifest itself in art and thereby give the highest proof of its reality need not concern itself with the world, since the world can attain totality only in art.[2] It was, therefore, at least Hebbel's will to embody in his finished artistic creations the philosophic synthesis of his experience, and it is for this reason that any discussion of his orientation towards progressivism or conservatism must be based very largely upon an understanding of his dramas.

In Hebbel's view all life is a struggle of the individual with the whole,[3] a struggle that develops and reveals the individual's character.[4] It is a struggle that is integral to the life process itself, and finds its truest expression in the drama, in which is revealed the critical relation of the individual to the Idea: the individual is opposed to the Idea by virtue of an incomprehensible freedom, having escaped from the nexus of the Idea and yet remaining a part of it.[5] The drama exercises its real function only where there is such a problem,[6] and, when successful, is superior to philosophy in performing the task which is common to them both. Philosophy has really failed in its part of the common task, and has never demonstrated the inevitability of the process of individuation, whereas art has always been able to perform its part, which is to change the discord of individuation to harmony through the resolution of the individual in the Idea, so that the breach caused by the incomprehensible freedom of the individual is closed. The breach which is to be closed by art is a necessary consequence of the mere fact of individuation, the original sin which is integral to every human being by virtue of his mere existence as such.[7] Life is the attempt of the rebellious part to tear itself loose from the Whole, an attempt which can be successful only as long as the strength lasts which the part has usurped in making itself free of the Whole.[8] The original sin of individuation has nothing to do with the goodness or wickedness of a person, is in no way dependent upon the tendency or quality of will, but only the existence of the individual constitutes the transgression, which may, on the human level, have the guise of morality as well as immorality. This is the only transgression with which the highest form of the drama is concerned and it is immaterial for the drama whether the hero perishes in a laudable or reprehensible endeavor. In fact, the tragedy of a laudable endeavor is the more poignant and cathartic spectacle.[9] There is only one necessity: that the world be maintained. The welfare of the individuals in the world is of no consequence. The evil things they do, since these things constitute a threat to the world, must be punished, but there is no reason why they should receive compensation for the misfortunes they suffer.

The respect in which Hebbel considers art as having been successful, in contrast to philosophy, is in a kind of re-creation of the cosmic process by which the individual is reabsorbed by the Idea. Actually, to be sure, the endeavor of the part to be free of the Whole is futile. Just as the air supplies us with vital physical [chemical] substances, so the spirit breathes and has its being in God. Every thought, every feeling is a drawing of the breath. It is folly to think that it is possible to detach oneself from God. To commit sin is about the same as a wilful attempt to stop breathing: the air will force its way, so to speak, of its own accord.[10] Yet, as we have seen, sin, in the particular metaphysical sense of the present context, is inevitable simply because the individual does and can exist only as an individual. If the individual denies itself, then its living is only a dying, an unnatural and useless withering. However, although the individual exists only as such, it none the less has no duty more sacred than to try to tear itself out of itself, for only in this way can it attain to a consciousness or even to a sense of itself.[11] The resolution of the discord of individuation is accomplished in the drama, which dissolves the basic dualism when it becomes too poignant, and a reconciliation is effected between the part and the Whole. The reconciliation, and this means the tragic elimination of the individual through reabsorption by the Idea, can take place in either of two ways: it may be incomplete, and then the individual goes down defiant and unbroken, which means that the form of individuation that he represents will reappear, or else it is complete and the individual, in perishing, has gained a purified insight into its relation to the Whole, and passes away in peace.[12]

The original cause of individuation, which it would be the task of philosophy to determine, is unfathomable. The drama passes over this problem, accepting the fact of individuation as a prime condition of life, and makes no attempt to reach a solution. It is here that the drama and the ultimate mystery are lost in one and the same night: even though the metaphysical breach is closed, why did it have to occur at all? To this question Hebbel never found the answer and believed that no one will ever find it who asks it in real seriousness.[13]

An examination of Hebbel's plays will have to be concerned with the problem of the guilt or relative justification of the tragic characters and of their antagonists, as well as with the nature of the conflict and the opposing forces. As regards the concept of guilt, Hebbel seems to have been rather inconsistent: on the one hand, he speaks of the guilt or sin of individuation and, on the other, seems to feel that the highest tragic effect is reached when there is no guilt and the individual perishes through some praiseworthy endeavor. The guilt which enhances the tragic effect through its absence is ordinary guilt on the human level, the kind of guilt associated with the wrong done one human being by another. This kind of guilt is irrelevant to tragedy. Tragic or dramatic guilt, unlike personal sin in Christian belief, is not a functon of the direction or intent of human will, but is a direct function of the will itself. Dramatically, it is a matter of complete indifference whether the hero perishes while doing good or evil. Dramatic guilt alone is the concern of tragedy, the highest form of art.

The twofold use of the term guilt involves an obvious difficulty or confusion, stemming, on the one hand, from Hebbel's particular use of the term in the sense of metaphysical guilt, and, on the other, from the traditional sense of the certain flaw in character of which Aristotle speaks in the thirteenth chapter of the *Poetics*, a moral defect in the tragic hero which, although it may be out of proportion to his tragic fate, may nevertheless be considered the cause of the hero's involvement in the mortal struggle with forces which defeat him. Because the term tragic guilt or tragic flaw is liable to such a misinterpretation, it seems desirable to suggest a term to replace it that will not carry the note of moral censure and yet will suggest the idea of some trait of character, some circumstance, or perhaps conjunction of circumstances, which lets tragic forces in upon the tragic persons in a play to destroy them. At some point there is a crack in the hero's armor, not necessarily a weakness, not necessarily a virtue; it is merely a point where the tragic forces are assembled and concentrated, where they are brought to a focus and burn through. This point may be called the tragic focus and will be so called in the present discussion. To be sure, in some instances in Hebbel's plays, for example, Meister Anton or Agnes Bernauer, it would be hard to speak of a tragic focus within the individual, since the whole being of such a character is the focussing point of the tragic force.

It will also be necessary to consider carefully what the nature of the tragic force is in Hebbel's drama, who or what the antagonists are, and to what extent the antagonists are justified relatively to one another. To anticipate a bit, examples of relevant, specific questions that must be answered are: Are the opponents in *Agnes Bernauer* Albrecht and Agnes on the one hand and Duke Ernst on the other? Are Agnes and Ernst equally in the right by standards of human morality, and, if so, does this mean that Ernst is justified and Agnes must be sacrificed only because of the fact that the conflict took place at a particular time and place in history and that nothing more is required than a shift of historical perspective in the direction of social progress for Agnes to be fully justified, and presumably, untouched by tragedy?

In the essay, *Mein Wort über das Drama*, Hebbel points out that it is not his conception that the tragic conflict is on the level of the individual human opponents. This essay was written in reply to Professor J. L. Heiberg, an authority of some note in Copenhagen on aesthetic and philosophical matters, who had made an attack on a somewhat earlier essay of Hebbel, *Ein Wort über das Drama*. Heiberg had written that there was reason to feel that Hebbel abstracted life from the objective forces which determine it with the result that his drama presents mere individuals quite detached from the eternal principle. Hebbel indignantly denies that this is true: his use of the terms transgressing individual (*Einzelheit, die nicht Mass zu halten weiss*) and guilt (*Schuld*) imply the existence of a principle which can be sinned against. Sin is not a term which is applicable to the relation of one individual to another but implies a transcendent principle. An individual can be sinned against by other individuals only if he is the representative of such a transcendent principle, and the justification of opposing individuals is in proportion to the strength which they derive from the transcendent principle they embody.[14] Hebbel's conception is, therefore, that in his drama it is possible to speak only of metaphysical justification of the opponents and this necessarily implies that the tragic conflict is not on the level of individual human opponents. Thus, the tragic hero may have a human enemy but the Adversary is always God.

The tragic conflict of individual and Idea, that is, of man and God, is particularly evident in times of flux and it is only in times of flux that great drama can be written: it is the function of the drama, as the highest form of art, to represent the critical relation of the individual to the Idea, a relation which becomes apparent in its problematic aspects in the transition from one epoch of history to another. This does not, however, imply that the dramatist is limited to portraying such times of transition, for then the scene of all great dramas would have to be laid either in Greece at the time of the great tragic poets, or in western Europe, particularly England, at the time of Shakespeare, or in Europe in the nineteenth century, that is, at the time of Hebbel. Before the nineteenth century there have been two great historical crises. One was in the Greek world when the dialectic of the pagan drama subordinated the individual to Fate, and the other was in the emerging Protestant world when Shakespeare's drama emancipated the individual, admitting no limits to his expansive power, so that Shakespeare's characters, so far as they are men of action, eliminate every living being about them, or, so far as they are men of ideas, would by means of the most daring and terrifying questions eliminate God from the world. This Hebbel calls putting the dialectic in the individual. The third possibility is to put the dialectic in the Idea and this is the process which Hebbel believes Goethe began and did not finish and is the great problem of the nineteenth century.[15] This leads to an examination and analysis of the Idea, an attempt to make it reveal its true nature, not with the hope of changing it, which is impossible, but with the hope of establishing morality on a true metaphysical basis. According to this thoroughly conservative point of view nineteenth-century man does not want new and unique institutions but only a better foundation for those already existing. He wants to have them supported by nothing but morality and necessity, which are identical, and thus gain their own peculiar and inherent center of gravity.[16] From what we already know about Hebbel's vision of the world, it is apparent that the attainment of a metaphysical basis for morality can be possible only through the individual's gaining an insight into the nature of his relation to the Idea: when a human being comprehends his relation to the universe under the aspect of inevitability, he has completed his development and has actually ceased to be an individual, for the concept of this inevitability, the capacity to attain to it, and the strength to adhere to it, is the universal principle embodied in the individual, wipes out all unjustified egotism, and frees the spirit from death by anticipating it in the essentials.[17] The perfect individual must therefore be one with the Idea, that is, surrender his individuality. The fact that we have knowledge of ourselves is the reason that we do not have complete knowledge of God. The highest beings have no knowledge of themselves but of God only.[18]

Knowledge of herself which obscures her vision of God might be a formula for expressing the tragic focus of Judith,[19] the heroine of the first of the plays which fall entirely within the period of sharp fluctuation already discussed (p. 5 above). From the moment she first hears of him Holofernes threatens to drive her God out of Judith's heart: "I would like to see him," she says, and is immediately dismayed by a desire which intuition tells her is sinful. For three years she has been living in a strange sort of widowhood: her husband had died some months after her wedding without ever having known her as his wife. Some terrible force had kept him from approaching her on their wedding night and they had lived together in an unconsummated union. Judith had thus been singled out and set aside to be used as an instrument in the working out of a divine purpose, to save her people from conquest and extermination by Holofernes. But the very experience which made it possible for her to become the instrument of God's will also made her peculiarly liable to become estranged from God. In fact, the estrangement was a necessary part of the instrumentality: the only access she could have to Holofernes to bring down divine retribution upon him was as a woman, an access which could be suggested to her only by her personal desire. Thus, the very first step she undertakes is a step towards tragedy, regardless of the outcome of her undertaking; had Holofernes responded to her womanliness as matching his power and raised the siege of Bethulia for her sake, even so the end would have been tragic for Judith, since Holofernes would have come between her and her God. Holofernes, however, sees in her only a means of satisfying his sensual appetites, a rather more stimulating intoxicant than wine, and uses her as such. Judith's deed, which saves her people and thus serves the divine purpose, springs directly from her outraged personal feelings which force her to kill the only man she might have loved, who alone could have given meaning to her life. Indeed, it is only the sense of outrage which gives her the strength to commit the deed, which, as she feels afterwards, is the worst crime of woman, and for which she desires to be punished. She exacts a promise from the elders to kill her if she requires death from them, but makes her life or death dependent upon the will of her divine Adversary: if God does not let her bear the child who must one day demand a reckoning of her, she can live. The obscurity of the issue is a consequence of the curse which rests upon humanity: the individual, even though he may in holy zeal consecrate himself as a sacrifice to God, is never a pure sacrifice, for sinful death is the necessary consequence of sinful birth; even though Judith falls for the sins of all, in her own consciousness she falls only for her own sin. For this reason the ending must be inconclusive, permitting either outcome.[20]

Judith and Holofernes are more than individuals, they are also representatives of their people. Judith is the dizzy peak of the people which believed it was in direct personal relation with God. Holofernes represents the excess of cruelty of a polytheism so extreme that it takes the last step and deifies the individual man, conceives the idea of a God to be born of mankind. Holofernes not only has this conception of the Man-God, he believes he is the Man-God. The heathen, polytheistic manifestation of the Idea, represented by Holofernes, and the Hebrew, monotheistic manifestation of the Idea, represented by Judith, conflict, at a time when mankind has not yet reached the point at which direct intervention by God would be unnecessary.[21] It is the direct intervention of God which constitutes the active tragic force of the play, destroying both Holofernes, who is in opposition to God in His monotheistic manifestation, and Judith, who is His instrument. Holofernes, the extreme concentration of heathen brutality, to which the notion of conquering itself is alien, through his mere existence challenges the Adversary and is defeated by means of the woman whom the Adversary has set aside as a weapon that will shatter even as it deals the mortal blow. Despite the fact that not only the individual that is opposed to the triumphant form of the Idea, but also the individual that serves this form of the Idea is destroyed, the play represents a progressive point of view: the brute strength of polytheism, having gone through an orgy of destruction and unable to control itself, could end only in the self-destruction for which Holofernes longs. Since, in Hebbel's view, the one necessity is that the world maintain itself, this form of the Idea must be replaced by a new form, which will allow life to go on.

If knowledge of self which obscures her vision of God might be a formula for expressing Judith's tragic focus, knowledge of God through perfect saintliness might be a formula for expressing the tragic focus of Genoveva.[22] Hebbel comments upon her character in his diaries:[23] her suffering is merely external and at the same time it justifies and develops the deepest elements of her nature, the religious elements: she is a completely Christian character, who is not consumed but transfigured by being burned at the stake; as far as she is concerned, the main intention of the play is to show how she attains to the same relationship to God as she once had to her husband, that for her profane love was always sacred love which had not become aware of itself. In the play itself Genoveva is almost identified with God, the only line of demarcation between them being Genoveva's finite existence. This almost complete identity is brought out not only in the final episode of sanctification in the epilogue,[24] which was written at the beginning of Hebbel's final conservative period (p. 15 above), but also in the play itself, which belongs to the same period as Judith (p. 5 above) through the circumstance that Golo, having tempted Providence by scaling the tower which it had been certain death to climb, then repeatedly tempts Genoveva in the same way. That is, climbing the tower is a kind of metaphysical experiment:[25] having a premonition of the monster that he would show himself to be, he hoped by this to challenge God to doom him and let him fall to his death, the more so since the feat was so dangerous that Golo's success in climbing it and returning in safety signified to him not only that God had not struck him down but had even sustained him,[26] a proof that it was his destiny to be a villain.[27] It is the same kind of decision that he repeatedly demands of Genoveva, feeling that it is God who speaks to him through her mouth:[28] he asks her to speak for God and say whether a person who feels that he must inevitably become a monstrous criminal has the right to take his life[29] and when she refuses to reply, by insisting that her silence will mean her consent to his suicide, he forces her to bid him to remain alive, just as in the prison scene he forces her to pour out the poisoned wine he has prepared for himself, that is, take a positive step to prevent his death, even though taking this step will impel him to press on to the ultimate in his infamous endeavor to possess or kill her. Despite, or rather, because of being God's representative on earth, Genoveva is not immune to extreme tragic suffering. To any other woman there would have been one, perhaps two ways to avert the torture inflicted upon her by Golo, the separation from her husband, the fatal hardships of living in the wilderness. The one, the baser and less certain way, would have been to yield to Golo or pretend to, lay a trap for him, and either unmask him before her faithful Drago and the others or kill him as Judith killed Holofernes. The other, the certain way, would have been to consent to his suicide. Neither alternative, of course, could be possible for the pure instrument of God's will. In the epilogue, Genoveva, having been perfected in saintliness through her suffering, appears to her husband in order to receive justification in the sight of the world, and having gained insight into the nature of her relation to the Idea has so far ceased to be an individual in her anticipation of being reabsorbed into God through death (cf. p. 28 above) that she prays for only seven days of life together with Siegfried before her final dissolution.

If Genoveva's tragic focus lies in the fact that she is, as an individual, so nearly at one with God as to be His representative and instrument on earth and, being an instrument, must necessarily experience the wielder of the instrument as the Adversary, Golo's tragic focus is of an entirely different kind. His whole being is a challenge to the Adversary, from the moment that the vision of perfect goodness and beauty arouse in him unlimited evil. In a passage omitted from the play Golo was to have said that under the aspect of the eternal the individual is already everything that he can become, and in his diaries[30] Hebbel makes the additional comment upon this idea that in the sight of God the sins of individuals against each other will not count, but only the sins against the Idea itself and in this regard actual and merely potential sins are completely identical. Golo's villainy is, indeed, identical with his highest capacity, and once quickened by Genoveva's perfect beauty which he desires and may not possess, it must manifest itself in a necessary succession of ever more terrible forms.[31] Golo is aware of this fatal compulsion to attain to a full realization of his potentialities; he knows that there is only one way to forget that one is a robber: to become a murderer, then a parricide, and after that there is nothing left but to destroy the world, to murder God Himself.[32] His mere existence threatens God. It is because he becomes aware of this in his passion for Genoveva, which makes him disloyal to Siegfried even in the first stirring of desire, that in climbing the tower he demands a divine judgment whether he is to live or die. This same judgment he demands of Genoveva, and he receives the same sentence: he must live. By constantly retreating, so to speak, God allows the rebellious individual to continue his dreadful advance, from which there is no turning back for Golo save by the impossible denial of self, and which must end, when he believes he has encompassed Genoveva's death, in terrible self-castigation and destruction: he tears out his eyes and prepares to meet slow death in the wilderness. Golo's slaying by Caspar is a merciful release from life, to which the Adversary had doomed him in retribution for his revolt.

Golo is condemned to live by the same tragic force, the will of God, which requires suffering of Genoveva. If it is true that Genoveva's destiny must be fulfilled so that Golo's hell may be complete,[33] it is also true that Golo's tragic unfolding of original sin must take place so that Genoveva may attain the same relation to God that she once had to Siegfried.[34] Both Golo and Genoveva are crushed in the accomplishment of a cosmic process. Genoveva, the frail and finite representative of God, says to Golo: If God protects the youth's [i.e.Golo's] sacrilegious boldness, it is a sign that His eye has already seen the day when He will have need of the man.[35] Revelation of the cosmic process is the inner purpose of the play, its idea, which Hebbel felt to be also the source of its weakness. He wrote in his diary:[36] "The flaw of the play is the flaw of its idea, the worst that it can have; this idea is the Christian one of expiation and atonement by saints." The flaw lies in the fact that this idea does not permit the play to be the tragedy of Genoveva but it must be her glorification. For this reason Genoveva cannot and may not be in the forefront of attention[37] and Golo is actually the main character. This division of interest and the split in the unity of the play which Hebbel realized and which caused him concern,[38] does tend to detract from the revelation of the cosmic process.[39] At the same time, however, it is most characteristic for Hebbel's conception of the tragic that Golo as well as Genoveva is each necessary for the consummation of the other's destiny: Genoveva is the instrument which God allows Golo to use to destroy himself; Golo is the instrument through which Genoveva attains perfect saintliness and ultimate unity with God.

In the tragic attainment of perfect saintliness Genoveva serves a great cosmic purpose. What this purpose is, is revealed by the spirit of the murdered Drago who appears to pronounce doom on the witch Margareta, the incarnation of evil: in the beginning God promised never to exterminate the sinful human race if every thousand years only one individual should prove worthy. The critical time is now at hand and it is Genoveva who can avert the punishment through her purity and suffering. In seven years her time of trial will be over, she will be assumed into eternal glory and mankind will be saved.[40] The depravity and wickedness which threaten to provoke divine retribution are represented in various episodes and characters in the play: Margareta is the pure incarnation of evil; ordinary Christians have become so brutal that they wish to stone a Jew merely for having drunk from a fountain which a diseased dog might use with impunity; the various retainers in Siegfried's castle show an appalling brutality and readiness to consort with evil. It is an age which is ripe for a terrible crisis and can be saved only by the vicarious atonement of Genoveva, and this, as we have seen, Hebbel felt was the inner idea of the play.

The historical crisis lies in the conflict of Christianity and Islam. Although no exact indication of the time of the play is given by the play itself, the list of persons carrying only the notation, "The Poetic Age," Hebbel probably did have a rather definite time in mind. At any rate, less than a year after the completion of *Genoveva* he noted in his diary[41] that the battle at Poitiers where Charles Martell defeated Abd-er-Rhaman, the leader of the Moslems, occurred in 732 and that therefore the action of *Genoveva* takes place in that year.[42] The advance of the Moslems to Poitiers constituted a very serious threat to Christianity and in terms of Hebbelian tragedy would be one of the great historical crises in which opposing manifestations of the Idea contend for superiority. Victory of the Moslems would have meant the emergence of a new form of the Idea, which showed itself not only mightier but even worthier than the old form of the Idea or Christianity. The demonstration of the moral worthiness of Islam is the purpose of the episode of the returning knight, Tristan, who made a vow never to lift his sword against a Moslem because of his kind and humane treatment by Fatima, the daughter of the Moslem he had served as a slave. Despite this serious threat, the older form of the Idea or Christianity, is triumphant in *Genoveva*, and the old covenant, by which God promised to withold his punishment if one human being could withstand all tribulations and temptations, is renewed. The established order is upheld, no transition to a new stage is represented in *Genoveva*, the play is conservative.

The comedy, *Der Diamant*,[43] from the same period as the preceding plays (p. 5 above), is the story of a Jew who swallows a diamond he has stolen in order to keep it in his possession. He has reckoned without the cupidity and desires of a great many other people who will stop at nothing to obtain the diamond: because the Jew cannot produce the stone, he loses all human worth and autonomy, does not become the owner of a piece of property, but himself constitutes a piece of property. Each person in the play desires the stone for a different and characteristic reason and in his attempts to gain possession of it reveals his inmost character. The value of the diamond is not intrinsic: to some it represents release from poverty and the power to do good, to others it represents a means of satisfying greed, to others it is a symbol of the continuing power and welfare of the ruling dynasty and the state. Hebbel's conception of the significance of objects as symbols has already been touched upon in connection with the passage from his diaries about the paving blocks of the state (cf. p. 14) and will again be touched upon in connection with *Gyges und sein Ring*, where it is of great significance for the bearing it has upon the question under consideration in the present study: the veil, the sword, and the crown are symbols for enduring traditional values. The diamond symbol is a grotesque and comic inversion of the veil, sword, and crown symbol, and serves to illuminate the empty illusoriness and futility of earthly life. The mood of the comedy is too disillusioned, too skeptical of human values and ambitions to be either progressive or conservative.

A similar feeling of skepticism, disillusionment, disbelief in both past and future finds very serious and gripping expression in another play from the period of violent fluctuation outlined in the first part of this study (pp. 5-9, esp. 7-8), *Maria Magdalene*,[44] the drama through which Hebbel intended to regenerate middle-class tragedy by showing that crushing tragedy is possible even in the narrowest circle if the dramatist knows how to derive it from the proper elements, that is, elements which are inherent in this circle itself.[45] The narrow circle, to which all the characters in the play belong, is the lower middle class of society in Hebbel's own time. Not only do the characters belong to this class but they almost all unquestioningly accept its code of morality, its standards of values and behavior. With the partial exceptions of the secretary and Klara's brother Karl, they all so completely accept this moral code and identify themselves with this society that none of them seriously questions the necessity and appropriateness of his or her actions. As Hebbel writes[46] to the actress, Auguste Stich-Crelinger, the tragedy does not come from a conflict of the middle class with the upper class but from the obduracy of the patriarchal traditions of the middle class itself and its inability to adapt itself to a complicated situation, so that Klara's fate is occasioned by a trivial transgression and none the less grows to terrifying proportions.[47]

Klara's father, Meister Anton, is the central figure, completely identified with the moral code of which he and all the others are victims. A model of upright middle-class honesty and respectability, he is tyrannical in his home, intolerant in his dealings with everyone he does not consider respectable, not because he takes pleasure in wounding others, but because he is convinced that his moral duty prescribes extreme rigidity and that there is no other way of discharging the obligations he owes himself, his family, and society. His household is governed in all its details by specific regulations, none of them trivial: the hat belongs on the third nail, not the fourth, at ten-thirty it is time to be tired, before Martinmas no freezing, after Martinmas no sweating, thou shalt love and fear God—thus Karl sums up the rigid control from which he seeks to escape.[48] Meister Anton has developed all this grim discipline of himself and others as a protection against the jibes and censure of society. When telling Leonhard about his first master, Meister Gebhard, who took him on as an apprentice, gave him food and lodging instead of demanding to be paid, and occasionally sent him home to his impoverished and widowed mother with half a ham, tears come to his eyes, betraying that, deep within him there is still the sensitive nature, which was constantly and deeply wounded, as he says, by the sharp porcupine's quills that were directed inward, until he reversed them and made them point out.[49] The gruff and bitter manner, which others fear, however, has by no means made him independent of society, but, on the contrary, has made him still more completely subservient. He must conform and make his family conform to all the minutiae of middle-class conventions, so as to avoid being the object of pity or scorn.[50] He can, and has proved that he can, endure anything at all except disgrace. He says to Klara that disgrace would sever the nerve that holds him together.[51]

Klara knows this, therefore she does not doubt for an instant that Meister Anton will cut his throat, as he says he will, if it becomes evident that Klara is to bear an illegitimate child. Moreover, she does not seem to feel that he is wrong about this but acquiesces to his threatened action as necessary, even, perhaps, right, if her disgrace is revealed, and she is driven by only one purpose, to stave off the fatal disgrace by any means. Or rather, she is ready to resort to any means but one and that is to deceive Friedrich, the secretary, whom she has never ceased to love, and who, as he reassured her too late, also loves her. Thus, if Meister Anton is the victim of the moral code which he upholds, the same holds true with even greater poignancy for Klara. Even her original transgression stems from her endeavor to comply with what is expected of her. When Friedrich, the childhood friend whom she came to love and who she believed returned her love, left his home to complete his studies, he thereby in the estimation of the townspeople raised himself to a higher level of society where Klara could not follow him. When he stopped writing to her the village gossips began to mock her for still thinking of him and aspiring to be more than she was. Even her mother urged upon her the greater suitability of Leonhard, her social equal. Her own wounded feelings and the desire to show Friedrich that she was not entirely dependent upon him contributed a bit also to her resolution to accept Leonhard as her fiance.[52] Even the motives which led her to agree to Leonhard's demand that she demonstrate the solemnity of their betrothal by the only proof he could not doubt, to accord him nuptial rights before their marriage, did not involve a basic deviation from the accepted moral code. Seeing Friedrich at the dance made her acutely aware that the old love was not dead, so that Leonhard seemed to be asking no more than the legitimate assurance that she had been honest in betrothing herself to him. Besides, if she was honest in this, no risk was involved, scarcely even the moderate disapproval of society, which was quite prepared to tolerate such a license if only it was legitimized later.[53] If in Meister Anton the over-scrupulous regard for honor, the thing itself, is at least matched by his regard for the appearance of honor, this is not the case with Klara. True, she tries with utter desperation to save her father by keeping up the appearance of honor, but it is her fundamental honesty and personal integrity, the very flower of her code and Meister Anton's, which is the direct cause of her tragedy. To prove her honesty even to herself she had to consent to Leonhard's demand. To maintain her own integrity she cannot take the only way out of her tragic situation that remains open—to conceal her condition from Friedrich, marry him, and secure the appearance of legitimacy which would save her father and herself, at least, her outward self.

    To deceive Friedrich is the only way that she could take out of her tragic situation which she could be sure would save appearances. It is not, however, the only way out: there is another way or could have been, if Friedrich were not also controlled by the automatic reactions of convention. Even though he and Klara have just declared their love for each other, his first exclamation when she tells him of her condition is: "No man can get over that!"[54] It is this that seals Klara's doom. The hope she was beginning to conceive that in Friedrich love and compassion might prove powerful enough to enable him to conquer his natural dismay for her sake is dashed to the ground and there remain only two things for her to do: implore Leonhard to marry her, and, this failing, take her life in a way that would seem to be an accident. Friedrich's response seals his own doom also: he goes to kill Leonhard in a duel, so that the one person who knows about the situation will not remain alive to relish his knowledge and share it with others. The duel is fatal to both participants and in his dying moments, as he speaks with Klara's father and realizes that Klara has taken her own life, Friedrich sees also that he had it in his power to save them all by brushing aside the overrigid system of morality and convention which has claimed as its victims the very people who have done everything to uphold it.

This rigid system of morality and convention is, of course, the current embodiment of the Idea. In *Maria Magdalene,* however, there is not, as there is in the other plays discussed hitherto, a rival form of the Idea which threatens the position of the established form, but, as has been pointed out, the tragic discord is inherent in prevailing conditions. None of the characters champions or even represents a different conception of morality: the secretary realizes that the old system is at fault but dies because he conforms to it; Karl merely wishes to run away from something he doesn't like, but he really stands for the same thing in a brutalized form; "When Father isn't here your brother is your guardian," he cries as he snatches Leonhard's letter out of Klara's hand;[55] even Leonhard, base and worthless as he is, has no sense of being in conflict with his society and seeks merely to secure an assured place in it for himself. Klara, except for her transgression, would be a pure and noble embodiment of the Idea, and Meister Anton is the Idea incarnate in individual form. When we then consider that it is Meister Anton from whom emanates the force which drives them all, himself included, to tragedy or ruin, it becomes clear that this means that the principle of self-destruction is lodged in the prevailing form of the Idea. The most complete objectivation of this form of the Idea would leave no room for the individual, which, as we know from our consideration of material from the diaries and letters, must exist in order that the Idea may have life. Since the only necessity is that the world maintain itself, the rigid middle-class form of the Idea is ripe for a change, and there are indications in the play that a change is coming: the increasing literacy among the very young is undermining the authority of the older generation which does not have facility in reading and writing;[56] even Karl, who is not sensitive enough to question the system, seeks to escape from it; the dying secretary understands that Anton bears the responsibility for the entire tragedy. Even so the play can scarcely be called progressive: the symptoms of change do not indicate the coming of a worthier and higher form. Karl is brutal, Friedrich ineffective, and Meister Anton, who no longer understands the world, is stricken but unbowed, baffled and unyielding. He has gained no insight into his relation to the Adversary.

In *Julia*,[57] begun toward the end of the period of sharp fluctuation and completed in the very short period of optimistic progressivism (pp. 5 and 11), Hebbel made another attempt at direct criticism of contemporary society and, in a sense, repeated the basic situation of *Maria Magdalene*. In *Julia* it is Julia's father, Tobaldi, who is an almost exact parallel to Meister Anton, being, if anything, even more extreme, even more unyielding, even less aware of his relation to the Absolute and of its destructive rigidity. Julia herself, however, is not an exact parallel to Klara, because the father of her illegitimate child is Antonio, the man she loves. He has been prevented from making her his wife by a serious wound which had been inflicted upon him by the rebellious brigands whose leader he has been. In Antonio, the robber's son, Hebbel wished to portray the hopeless lot of a person who was born outside the pale of society,[58] thus exposing what, on the basis of his experience in Italy, he took to be one of the major ills of his time, namely brigandage, a form of life in which the individual has no choice but to revolt against society. That is, if society is so constituted as to make large scale brigandage inevitable, this points to a serious defect in the form in which the Idea is realized. A third serious defect to which Hebbel wished to point was libertinism or decadence. This social evil is embodied in Count Bertram whose excesses have caused his physical ruin. Logically enough, it is Bertram who is sufficiently emancipated from the tyranny of an over-rigid moral code to take the step which the secretary in *Maria Magdalene* was unable to take, offers a means of salvation to the woman whose life is threatened because of her transgression against the social code: Bertram offers Julia the name and position of being his wife. Thus Bertram through voluntary recognition of his guilt surrenders himself completely to the moral Idea and sacrifices his rights as an individual,[59] in this way closing the gap between the individual and the Absolute.

It is true that *Julia* is unsuccessful: Hebbel allowed himself to overestimate the significance of what he had observed in Italy, taking superficial ills of society to be fundamental. Not only that, the main characters, Julia, Antonio, and Bertram, represent such divergent and incongruous problems that the whole action seems artificial, unconvincing, and contrived. None the less, the play has an interesting bearing upon the problem of progressivism and conservatism in Hebbel and discloses an unrelieved pessimism and disillusionment: the successful opposition to the form of society which is responsible for the at least threatened tragedy of a Julia and an Antonio comes from a form represented by Bertram, which has obtained liberation and metaphysical reconciliation at the expense of making physical propagation of the individual impossible. Is decadence the answer to ruthless convention? If so, it is an answer which gives very little hope for the future.

Just as little hope for the future is held out by the other play which Hebbel based upon his experiences in Italy, *Ein Trauerspiel in Sizilien*,[60] but which was written during that brief period during which he seemed almost wholly committed to belief in social progress (p. 11). It represents the terrifying aspect of the police-state, the agents of which may be corruptible and evil, and also the extremes of the problem of possession and property.[61] The rich Gregorio has promised to cancel Anselmo's ruinous debt to him in return for Anselmo's daughter Angiolina in marriage. Angiolina and her lover Sebastiano, knowing only that Anselmo opposes their marriage, resolve to elope and be married secretly. Angiolina comes first to the meeting place, is robbed by two gendarmes, who then, largely to impress each other with their ferocity and to avoid being found out as robbers, kill Angiolina. When Sebastiano comes they resolve to accuse him of the crime and nearly succeed in convincing Gregorio and Anselmo, but the truth is revealed by a fruit-thief who had seen the whole affair from a tree in which he had hidden. This short play is intended as a tragi-comedy, which, according to Hebbel's theory, is the result whenever a tragic destiny is revealed in an untragic form, where the antagonists are, on the one hand, a human being struggling but going down to defeat, and, on the other, not the justified moral force, but a quicksand of foul conditions which swallows up a thousand innocent victims. This, he felt, was the only adequate means of representing many contemporary events.[62]

Thus the impression left by these three plays of criticism of contemporary social conditions is one of profound pessimism. If contemporary conditions are so bad as to disintegrate because of their own inherent weakness, there is still no reason to hope for anything much better soon. The woes of the individual are too poignant to leave much opportunity for appreciating the beauty of a metaphysical reconciliation, even though the placid surface of the Absolute is restored when the agitating ripples of the individual have subsided.[62a]

Herodes und Mariamne,[63] which was begun in the short period of progressivism and completed in the time of transition to conservatism (p. 11), is still more terrifying in its representation of ineluctable doom than the last three plays discussed, but it is, however, much less pessimistic and negative: whereas in *Maria Magdalene*, for instance, the feeling is that there is no star to guide humanity out of a hopeless situation, in *Herodes und Mariamne* the sense of hopelessness is mitigated by the historical perspective. Take this away and there would be little to choose between them in point of unrelieved pessimism. In both, the characters move in orbits fixed in the nature of their social systems, they proceed along astronomical paths predetermined by the Adversary. What Hebbel said [64] about the earlier play, that actually all the characters, even Leonhard, who is so base as to have no conception of anything finer, are in the right, and that it is therefore the mono-ideological petrifaction of life from which the whole disaster springs, he substantially repeats about *Herodes und Mariamne* in a letter[65] to Eduard Janinski: the characters are all in the right, at no point do they end up in wickedness, and their destiny proceeds from the fact that they are precisely the characters they are and no others. This, applied to Herodes himself, is rather amazing: how is it possible to maintain that the despot who ordered the death of all the infants in Bethlehem was not wicked? But there can be no doubt about Hebbel's intention: in a letter to H. T. Rötscher he is perhaps even more emphatic in expressing his wish to let nothing in the play be dependent upon moods and decisions which have only a relative basis in the characters and relationships and can be one way or the other.[66] Everyone who is human, he says, must feel the necessity of Herodes' resolution, which is the efficient cause of everything and which seems to be not merely mysterious, in the sense of arising out of the indecipherable primeval depth of personality, but actually fantastic. The inflexible necessity, which is in this sense Herodes' justification, lies in the fact that what is ordinarily taken as background, the factors of time and place, rigidly determine the scope of action left to each character in the play. This is parallel to *Maria Magdalene*: Meister Anton embodies the killing strictness of the moral code: if the individual moves at all he must move in a certain way and this means death and ruin. But Meister Anton as an individual is just as absolutely bound by the rigid system he embodies and all real life is squeezed out of him by it. Herodes also embodies the prevailing form of the Idea: oriental despotism in its extreme disregard for individual life, but as an individual he is just as inevitably crushed as was any of his victims. The particular actions and events of *Herodes und Mariamne,* which seem so improbable and incredible, even though they are satisfactorily documented, it was Hebbel's intention to show as inevitably proceeding out of the general conditions of the world, of the people, and the age; it was his intention to derive Herodes' delirium from the atmosphere he breathed and this, the atmosphere, from the vaporous volcanic earth on which he stood.[67]

The volcanic earth on which Herodes must maintain his kingdom is, indeed, both fiery and unstable. He is, of course, only a vassal king, his power completely dependent upon the interests of Rome and the whims of Antonius, who established him, perhaps partly because of a certain esteem for him but mostly because of the tribute Herodes pays which enables Antonius to live in magnificence with Cleopatra.[68] The Roman captain Titus is stationed in Jerusalem, ostensibly as Herodes' subordinate and commander of the legions which support him, but actually Titus will serve him only as long as Herodes can continue to hold the kingdom together for Rome. He can and does hold the kingdom together by virtue of his extraordinary personal gifts of resolution and ruthlessness as well as by virtue of the fact that he is allied through marriage with the great line of the Maccabees. This hold upon the people is less firm than it was, however, because Herodes is interested in not merely holding the kingdom together but in creating a power which will be of some consequence in the world. To do this he feels he must break the religious isolationism of the Jews.[69] Thus, although Herodes does embody oriental despotism in its ruthless disregard for human life, he is, and in this respect he is not the unqualified embodiment of the traditional form of the Idea that Meister Anton is, a kind of social reformer also and has left the stage of despotism represented by the satraps, at whose court human beings served as clocks and living torches.[70] The religious conservatism of the people is exploited by Sameas, the Pharisee, fanatical in his worship of the letter of the law and implacable in his hatred of the Romans and Herodes. He has fomented a conspiracy in which even an ineffectual blind man has a part merely out of hatred for Herodes. The conspiracy, however, flares into open revolt during the regency of Joseph and must be put down by violence by Titus and his soldiers. But Sameas in prison and a martyr is an even greater menace to Herodes than he was as a free man: he prophesies in his torment and foretells the birth of the Child who will rule forever.[71] However, the danger to Herodes from Sameas not only threatens his relations with his people but is inextricably bound up with the dangers that threaten him in his own household, for Sameas is in league with Herodes' mother-in-law, Alexandra, each seeking to use the other as an instrument to attain private ends. Alexandra is Herodes' most dangerous enemy: not only does she stir up popular revolt through Sameas and smuggle spies into Herodes' service[72] but she tries by every device she can conceive to induce Antonius to turn against him. Except for Mariamne Herodes has no one whom he can love and trust: his mother is of no significance and his sister Salome is so dominated by hatred of Mariamne that she has kissed her only once, when Mariamne seemed to be on the point of death.[73] In all this welter of venomous hatred Herodes, the man, is sustained by one thing, his love of Mariamne and hers of him. It is the one thing he really has, the one thing he must keep at any cost, the best thing about him, and also his weak point, the tragic focus of his individuality. When the play opens we see him, so to speak, at the stage where every move that is left for him to make in the cosmic game of chess exposes both him and the queen he seeks to save to the impersonal malice of the Adversary.

The decisive move in the game has been made just before the action of the play begins. Alexandra, scheming to find new ways to ruin Herodes, has had Aristobolus, her son and Mariamne's brother, consecrated to the office of high priest, the spiritual headship of the state, the equal and, under the right circumstances, the rival of the kingship. Aristobolus, being a thoughtless boy, had let himself be used in his mother's schemes to draw popular support away from Herodes and become a figure-head whom Antonius might use to replace Herodes. Alexandra had gone farther and sent a portrait of Aristobolus to Antonius in order to arouse in him a passion to possess Mariamne, whose resemblance to her brother was very great. The danger had become so intense that Herodes was forced to have Aristobolus killed in a simulated accidental drowning. It is to answer before Antonius to the charge of murder that Herodes must leave for Alexandria. It is the death of Aristobolus that now threatens to take from him his only real possession, Mariamne's love, and he in turn takes the perverse and desperate measure to insure that she will never belong to another, but which even more surely takes her from him forever: fearing that the death of Aristobolus has estranged Mariamne, Herodes wants from her the assurance, an oath, that she will not become another man's wife, that she will die, if he does not return. Mariamne, who feels that her enjoyment of Herodes' absolute trust has already been violated by Herodes' feeling it necessary to pretend mourning at Aristobolus' death, since she was not blind to the peril to the state which her brother represented,[74] finds herself quite incapable of taking such an oath, indeed, affronted by the demand. But Herodes cannot see that in order to retain what he most cherishes he must be ready to let it go and leaves Joseph, his regent, with the secret order to kill Mariamne, should Herodes die, in order to prevent her from ever belonging to Antonius. Thus, although the play is in a certain sense a tragedy of love, as von Wiese maintains,[75] drawing the fire, intensity, and vividness of its characterization and the relentless poignancy of its movement from this source, it is scarcely, as von Wiese seems to feel, basically a tragedy of love and secondarily an historical tragedy, but rather the tragedy of love is completely conditioned by the historical guise which the great Adversary has assumed. It is not Herodes' love or the failure of it that drives the events inexorably to the tragic outcome, but it is the historical crisis which reveals or perhaps even causes the love of Herodes for Mariamne to be of a different order from the love which she can accept and return.

For Mariamne, who was no less exposed than Herodes to the cross-currents of hatred and the threat of insecurity, her love for Herodes and his for her must mean no less than for Herodes the center of life, whose inviolability alone makes it possible to endure the rest. Indeed, whereas for the man and the king love might be no more than the center of a life which is a constant unrelenting struggle, for this woman, even though a queen, love must fill life from the center to its utmost bounds: for Herodes love is something to have, for Mariamne it is something to be. Perhaps if Herodes had not been the king of Judea at that particular time in that particular situation he might have attained to a love of the same order as Mariamne's: at the crisis of decision when he is about to leave for the second time, he seems to have some sense of what the issue is,[76] but he cannot transcend the limits of his individual existence and so he cannot break off but instead gives fresh impetus to the chain of events which he began when he instructed Joseph to kill Mariamne in the event of his death at Antonius' hands. The limitations which he is thus unable to transcend are inherent in the form of the Idea which he represents: Oriental despotism with its norm of regarding the human being as a means of satisfying a purpose, desire, or whim. It is a love of this order against which Mariamne revolts, because she refuses to be a thing which the male and the sovereign can keep or discard as he might keep or discard a robe of state. She can forgive Herodes the killing of her brother,[77] she is ready to forget that he ever gave Joseph the fateful order, to believe that this happened in a delirium which was not symptomatic of his inmost self,[78] and so she rejoices when Herodes must leave her for the second time under the same conditions as the first, for now Herodes will have a chance to prove that his first act of pure despotism did not reveal his soul completely.[79] This deed which

Mariamne feels can perhaps be repeated but surely never outdone,[80] Herodes does, in fact, outdo when he seems only to repeat it. This time his regent is Soemus, a very different man from the ineffectual Joseph, and Herodes' most sincere and trusted friend. Herodes, knowing that the very order to kill Mariamne is fatal to the one who receives it,[81] none the less repeats it to Soemus, in whose case he cannot plead the alleviating circumstance of being blinded by sexual passion.[82] But Soemus as well as Mariamne represents a new order of things, will not tolerate being used as a tool by another human being, is just as deeply shocked at being forced to play a role which is fatal to him only because it suits Herodes' selfish purpose,[83] and intentionally reveals to Mariamne the secret which Joseph had been unable to conceal. Mariamne, who has just accused Soemus of being disloyal to his master, understands that Herodes has misused him just as he has misused her, has trampled upon the most sacred feeling of them both by reducing them to the status of thing.[84] Herodes' sin against Soemus added to his sin against Mariamne makes it plain beyond the possibility of doubt that a new conception of and belief in personality is stirring, not yet strong enough to triumph over the old, but, inasmuch as it reveals the bankruptcy of the old conception, portentous of a new order.[85] Both Soemus and Mariamne perish at Herodes' hands. But Mariamne brings about an ironical and tragic triumph over the force which kills her:[86] She, whom Herodes had thus degraded by making her the instrument of his desires, retaliates by making Herodes the unwitting instrument of her voluntary death:[87] she makes it appear that she rejoices at the report of Herodes' death, pretends to be what Herodes feared she might be, so that when he returns he orders her trial and execution. The new form of the Idea goes down defiant, a sign, as we have seen (p. 25, above), that it will reappear.

Both we and Hebbel's audience, viewing this crisis from the perspective of history, know that a new form of the Idea did appear, which stands for the belief in the sanctity of the individual. To make it clear beyond a doubt that this is the perspective from which the events of the play must be viewed, Hebbel lets us see the three Kings of the Orient following the star of Bethlehem.[88] Believing that the Infant-King they seek must have been born in Herodes' house they arrive in the palace at the exact hour of Mariamne's death, and then, learning that this is not the place, go on to Bethlehem in their search. Herodes, feeling that the Babe will pluck the crown from his head, issues the order for all children born within the year to be slain, the extreme and futile measure of the despot to make himself secure: the golden circlet he clutches with convulsive grasp is now, after Mariamne's death, a mere bauble, and the era of the Infant-King cannot be held back.

The fantastic fairy-tale comedy *Der Rubin*,[89] which belongs in the emergent phase of the final conservative period (p. 15), shows its inner relationship with *Herodes und Mariamne* by being, in a sense, an extended commentary on the difficulty, almost impossibility, of seeing that in order to retain what one most cherishes he must be ready to let it go. The idea was an old one with Hebbel: already in October or November 1836 he had written in his diary: "Wirf weg, damit Du nicht verlierst! ist die beste Lebensregel,"[90] and in 1843 he had published the prose-tale, *Der Rubin*, which related substantially the same story but without the emphasis on historical perspective which we find in the play. The fairy-tale comedy is, briefly, the story of a poor but very honest fisherman named Assad, who in Bagdad comes into possession of a wonderful ruby, which, as he learns afterwards, is the magic prison of the caliph's beautiful daughter. A wicked sorcerer has transformed her into this shape and set one condition for her liberation: that the possessor of the ruby throw it away. This, however, Assad does not know and yet he does fulfill the condition: ready to defend the possession of the ruby with his life, when he sees that he must inevitably lose it in death, he throws it into a river so that it will not fall into unworthy hands, and the princess is released from the gem.

In another respect also *Der Rubin* shows its relationship with *Herodes und Mariamne* and that is in its portrayal of oriental despotism. True, there is here no great historical crisis in the background. The political and social system of the caliphate disposes of human life and liberty with sovereign indifference and the caliph himself once in a fit of drunkenness killed one of his wives, the mother of the girl who has been transformed. This has caused the caliph to have a greater reverence for the individual than his minions,[91] in this respect representing a slightly advanced social view, although he himself feels that he used to be an innovator, breaking the law of the Koran in regard to wine, for instance, and that he has therefore been converted to strict observance of the law. On the other hand, there is no doubt that Assad's assumption of the throne as a reward for freeing the caliph's daughter does represent a step forward in social progress. As one of the submerged millions who has known poverty and the danger of arbitrary execution he will necessarily be unable to forget or disregard the miserable state of the submerged millions.[92] And, indeed, his first act as caliph is to liberate a man who has been arbitrarily put in chains and to state his intention to proclaim an amnesty. Assad's accession to power thus represents the emergence of a new social order, and the play is progressive.

A subject which had concerned Hebbel for a long time was his Moloch drama, of which he completed only two acts and left fragmentary sketches of the last three.[93] His long continued interest in it (cf. pp. 5 and 15, above) and his frequently stated hope to make it his masterpiece indicate that it must be included in any consideration of Hebbel's dramatic production. In no other play is the antagonism of the individual and the divine Adversary so concretely symbolized. The last surviving Carthaginian, Hieram, priest of Moloch, has brought his iron god to Thule, that is, primitive Germany, a land of savage hunters, who have neither religious belief nor any cultural skill. Hieram, having lost whatever faith he once may have had in Moloch, has determined to use the God to serve his own purpose: to subject the people of Thule to his will through arousing the sense of religious awe in them and to send them against Rome in retaliation for the destruction of Carthage. Up to a point Hieram is successful: Moloch becomes the dominant force in Thule and enables Hieram to rule the savages through Teut, the son of the old king, inasmuch as the younger Teut, particularly responsive to religious impulses, overthrows his father and becomes Hieram's zealous agent. Through belief in Moloch the people are led to change their rude manner of existence, to begin to dominate nature by tilling the soil and controlling its productivity, to establish social, cultural, religious institutions, to develop the rudiments of poetry and art. The completed acts of the drama show how Moloch was established in Thule by Hieram, the rest of the play was to show how Hieram, when he begins to attempt to exploit Moloch for his individual ends, is crushed by the iron Adversary he has raised up. He dies with the conviction that the divine principle even in its crudest form is more powerful than the mightiest man and that the individual must give way. But Hieram's achievements survive him, insofar as they merit survival, and at the end there is a glimpse into a world which grows more radiant with every day.[94] The play is plainly progressive, showing the origination of political and religious conditions which survive to the present day,[95] and showing in a mythico-poetic way the emergence of an ethnic group from barbarism into civilization.

In *Herodes und Mariamne* we have seen a tragedy of love completely conditioned by the historical guise which the great Adversary has assumed. Presumably the same thing is true of *Agnes Bernauer*:[96] it is surely a tragedy of love, and Duke Ernst, the human representative of the Adversary, in signing Agnes' death-warrant is sure, and his chancellor, Preising, against his will is forced to realize that no other course of action is possible. In fact, Ernst, like Golo, makes a "metaphysical experiment," the outcome of which decides Agnes' fate: he disinherits his son and names his nephew to the succession, but the nephew dies through the will of God and thus Agnes' doom is sealed.[97]

None the less the background factors of time and place do not in this play cast the events into a rigid and predetermined pattern: it is not the background factors, for example, which make the death of Ernst's nephew inevitable. This event, upon which the tragic outcome hinges, does not depend upon the historical guise which the Adversary has assumed, as does the death of Aristobolus in *Herodes und Mariamne*. And besides, the fact that Duke Ernst does not appear on the stage until the beginning of the third act introduces the factor of the state in visible form at such an advanced point in the action that the play does, as a matter of fact, fall into two parts, the tragedy of love and beauty and the political tragedy. It is suggestive that Hebbel's own comments about the play during the years that he was closer to it reveal a preponderance of interest in the political tragedy, and that it was written at the time when we have noticed a definite swing to conservatism in the diaries and letters (p. 15). Immediately upon completing the play he writes in his diary[98] that he counts it a great gain that he now understands the relation of the individual to the state as never before. This is an indication that in the very act of working on the play his insight into the nature of the political tragedy deepened, perhaps that his point of view shifted. Very soon after completing the play he writes to Dingelstedt[99] that his intention was to portray in the girl a being who evokes in the beholder a sense of wonder that a thing of such purity and delicacy can have emerged from the inertness of common humanity (... eine Lilie hinzustellen, der man es auf jedem Blatt noch ansieht, dass sie sich durch den Boden hindurch quälen musste ...), and in the duke a stainless representative of the highest power, who merely by exhibiting the sublime conception of duty subdues rebellious passion. Indeed, Hebbel came so deeply under the spell of his conception of the exalted position of the state that he could write to Friedrich Uechtritz[100] that he was completely on the side of the old duke and that it was the character of the duke that had aroused his interest in the whole subject. This does not, however, agree with a diary entry[101] from the time when he was just beginning the work of composing the play. Then he wrote that it seemed as though the subject of Agnes Bernauer had just been made to order for the idea which he had had for a long time of representing beauty in its tragic aspect, as being fatal through its mere existence. From an entry in his diaries[102] made a little over six years previously we know something about the shape which the tragedy of love and beauty took in his mind in the early stages. There he outlines the idea as the story of a very beautiful girl who has spent her first years in a cloister. Upon leaving it in complete ignorance of the inflammatory nature of her beauty she has the experience that wherever she goes she evokes passion and discord: rivals for her love hate each other, other women are jealous of her because even without intent or awareness she estranges them from their lovers. Finally, when the brother of the man she loves begins to plot his death, she is seized with terror of herself and seeks sanctuary in the cloister once more. The idea for the tragedy of love and beauty just outlined is characteristic of Hebbel and could well have been the basis of a different sort of tragedy, in which the heroine through her disastrous experiences attains an insight into the nature of her sin of individuation and, thereby, the kind of metaphysical reconciliation with the Adversary before death which Genoveva attains: the tragedy of beauty might thus have been a kind of repetition of the tragedy of saintliness. It is very interesting that about eleven years *after* the completion of *Agnes Bernauer* the original notion of the tragedy of love and beauty seemed to predominate in Hebbel's own evaluation of the play. He writes to Sigmund Engländer[103] that he never considered it a social drama, but that the Augsburg barber-surgeon's daughter always seemed so remarkable to him because her fate showed that the mere inactive existence of extreme beauty is by itself enough to set off a tragic conflict and that, therefore, in order to portray such a situation he had to make use of all the historical trappings. Thus it is at least interesting to contemplate the possibility that Hebbel was fundamentally interested in the tragedy of love and beauty and that the subject itself as well as Hebbel's growing sense of the value of tradition stimulated his interest in the political tragedy, with the resulting lack of unity that we have noted. This lack of unity has been noted by others, chiefly Heinrich Meyer-Benfey,[104] whose analysis and strictures, while over-severe and exhibiting a militant political liberalism, are penetrating and revealing. But it does not seem possible to accept his thesis that the artistic failings of the play are due to the fact that Hebbel identified himself with whatever characters, Albrecht and Agnes, or Ernst, he happened to be portraying.[105] However, the rift in conception that Meyer-Benfey exposes cannot be overlooked and is not really concealed by interpretations such as that of von Wiese,[106] which seeks to find the unity of the play in the tension between the tragedy of love and beauty and the political tragedy, which reveals a metaphysical rift in the Deity, or that of Hans M. Wolff,[107] who finds the unity in the figure of Albrecht as the pioneer representative of a new and better social order, a view which can find no support in the way Hebbel has organized his material, as, indeed, Wolff finally admits. Albrecht does have a certain unifying function in connecting the two tragedies, however, but it is not as the champion of progress. Still, it is probably necessary to come to the conclusion that the nuclei of two separate plays are more or less incompletely fused in *Agnes Bernauer*: on the one hand, the tragedy of love and beauty, which, following Hebbel's original impulse, might have come about as the result of civil war arising from rival claims to the throne which a child of Agnes could not legitimately occupy, and the tragedy of an incorruptible but human representative of the state, whose higher duty compels him to sacrifice what he holds most dear, even, by provoking war with his son, run the risk of losing both son and throne in order to keep them. Duke Ernst is a tragic character in scarcely a less degree than Agnes herself and if there is an esoteric unity in the play it lies probably in the circumstance that both Agnes and Ernst are crushed by the same Adversary, the one in defeat, the other in victory.

The parallel of Agnes with Genoveva is quite plain and, up to a point, consistent: in Genoveva, perfect saintliness, in Agnes, perfect beauty of both body and soul. What Albrecht says of her, that no man can look at her without incurring extreme danger[108] seems to be literally true: all the men of her own social circle from Theobald, her father's apprentice, to the superannuated Knippeldollinger are in love with her and she has no friends left among the girls of her own age. But Agnes arouses all these conflicting desires, hates, and jealousies without intending to do so, and, so genuine is her innocence that, when she is made aware of what has happened, her first impulse is to stay out of sight. The love which she and Albrecht feel for each other is spontaneous and absolute and permits of no compromises: neither one can tolerate the thought of an illicit relationship, and for each life without the other would be meaningless. Thus, as soon as Agnes and Albrecht have seen each other the threat of tragedy is invoked: the choice is between a life cancelled by renunciation and a marriage which challenges the established order of the state. If Albrecht and Agnes follow Ernst upon the throne of München-Bayern the result will be a long and bloody struggle for succession with the rival duchies of Ingolstadt and Landshut. There seems to be a way out, which Ernst chooses when he excludes Albrecht from the succession and names his nephew Adolph instead, but the metaphysical experiment fails: The collateral line of München-Bayern becomes extinct and the Adversary, after a respite of a brief two and a half years,[109] allows the fatal sequence of cause and effect to unfold. The instrument of execution, drawn up by the best jurists of the time, is now upon the death of Adolph readied for Ernst's signature. Before affixing his signature Ernst calls upon Preising to decide whether it is possible to save Agnes. Preising, who is shocked that Agnes must die only because she is beautiful and good,[110] is compelled to assent, but nevertheless takes it upon himself to hold open to Agnes one avenue of escape, namely that she repudiate her marriage. It is an avenue that she cannot take, since repudiation would brand as iniquitous her holiest possession. Thus Agnes is compelled by the perfection of her soul to choose submission to a sentence of death which had to be pronounced only because she did not shave her head and take the veil,[111] and the great Juggernaut passes over her.[112] Unlike Genoveva, however, Agnes does not attain an insight into her relation to the Adversary; in fact, she has no conscious relation to the Adversary whatever: she is the pure individual and her tragic focus is her entire being with its mysterious freedom.

Albrecht's tragedy is in its inception somewhat similar to the tragedy of Agnes: the imperious demands for individual fulfillment sweep aside any awareness of counter-demands imposed upon the individual by the universal forces. Albrecht's tragic focus is a love for Agnes so absolute that it makes him place his personal rights above the rights of his future subjects and he thus, unlike Agnes, who is passive, comes into active opposition to the Idea, going even so far as to head an army of rebellion. But no sooner has he taken his father prisoner than the act of tragic reconciliation begins to take place: an imperial herald and a papal legate begin to read ban and excommunication over him in the presence of the old duke, whose nobility of spirit has begun to reassert its claim to Albrecht's veneration. When Ernst talks to him of the duty which his high lineage has imposed upon him and promises him that full honors will be done Agnes as his deceased duchess, Albrecht bows to him as head of the state and representative of the emperor, but when Ernst gives him the ducal sceptre with the power to rule and the duty to sit in judgment upon his father after one year, Albrecht sinks to his knees before his father in token that he has experienced the tragic reconciliation.

Albrecht is the link between the tragedy of love and beauty and the political tragedy and, as such, prevents the play from falling apart. Through him the political tragedy is connected with the tragedy of love and beauty, which is thus made to contribute to the conservative tendency of the drama as a whole, to which many passages from Hebbel's diaries and letters, as already cited, attest. Duke Ernst, although he is the completely justified representative of the universal forces,[113] is no more immune to tragedy than Agnes or Albrecht. He is compelled to require the death of a person of whose personal innocence he is just as convinced as is his chancellor, Preising. In so doing he must inflict upon his own son an injury so keen that there is doubt in his mind whether Albrecht can survive, and he rejoices when Albrecht takes up arms against him, for this is a sign that rage has triumphed over despair and that Albrecht will not succumb to his grief.[114] He has resorted to these extreme measures in order to save what he has dedicated his life to and he goes even further, taking the step which Assad took but Herodes could not take: he gives up what he most cherishes—and himself too—in order to save it. Surrendering the ducal sceptre to Albrecht he knows that he is nearly broken by his experiences and by entering the monastery he anticipates death in its essentials. This step, too, is necessary for the complete and final triumph of the Idea which he represents, for it is this step which breaks the last remaining trace of resistance in Albrecht. The play exhibits the vindication and victory of conservative social forces. The form of the Idea which Ernst represents, unlike the prevailing form of the Idea in *Maria Magdalene,* at no point shows signs of turning rigid and lifeless. Indeed, far from destroying individual forms in its realization, it fosters and extends the possibilities of life for individual forms: it safeguards the life and happiness of myriads of nameless individuals.[115] Albrecht and Agnes experience tragedy because their love constitutes a challenge to the Adversary. Ernst, the instrument used by the Adversary to counter the challenge, triumphs insofar as he is identified with the Idea, but very nearly cracks under the strain of use.

The same kind of tragic process by which Albrecht achieves the metaphysical basis for morality through an insight into the relation of individual to Idea is represented in *Gyges und sein Ring*,[116] a play which upholds the eternal rights of ethical convention and tradition,[117] and is therefore in accord with the tendency to conservatism which marks the closing years of Hebbel's life (p. 15). According to a letter written to Uechtritz,[118] however, Hebbel was not conscious, while working on this play, as he was during the composition of the previous plays, of a certain background of ideas which framed the landscape, as he says, like a mountain-range; but he was fascinated merely by the story, which seemed so suitable for treatment as a tragedy, and only when the play was completed did he become aware of the idea of ethical convention as its central and governing idea. This judgment is borne out by a reading of the play itself, though it centers less upon the plot than the characters. No longer do the background factors of time and place determine the action, even the thoughts of the characters, as is true in *Herodes und Mariamne*, but they provide only a certain circumambience in which the action is more or less fortuitously imbedded. How fortuitously can be seen from the fact that the relation Rhodope, Kandaules, Gyges has already been encountered in Hebbel's work in many places, with many variations, and more or less completely: Judith, Holofernes; Genoveva, Siegfried, Golo; Klara, Leonhard-Anton, Friedrich; Julia, Tobaldi-Antonio, Bertram; Mariamne, Herodes, Soemus. The essential relations of the characters to one another and to the central idea, the idea of ethical convention, are not bound to any point in space and time, as Hebbel well knew.[119] The play presents a "timeless" problem, therefore one that can be considered modern as well as historical, in the costume of a semi-historical period that permits and makes credible the particular form of a more general conflict,[120] which reveals the relation of the individual to the idea of ethical convention. The culpable act of Kandaules which sets the tragic forces in motion and leads to the fatal conflict is consistent with the attitude of the Homeric Age toward woman: Helen passes from one possessor to another without diminishing in value or desirability; the Kandaules of Herodotus' story has the same attitude towards his wife as the owner of a valuable property which he feels he must exhibit to be sure of its worth.[121] Thus, Kandaules' act is conceivable only in such a setting, but its consequences and implications reach beyond the particular time and place, even into the realm of metaphysical universals.

It is the idea, not the specific form, of ethical convention which is central to the play,[122] and it is Rhodope, who has been in her chaste seclusion its unreflecting embodiment, leading a flower-like existence at her father's court in India, where, sitting underneath a plane-tree with a lily in her hand,[123] she seems to have been scarcely differentiated from the world which produced her. In a way she has been able to transfer her homeland to Lydia: she never leaves the palace and its gardens even when she might do so without reproach;[124] her veil, which she has worn at all times except when alone with her maidens or her husband[125] is a part of her being;[126] the doom decreed a dishonored woman, which made her shudder as a child, although it signifies her own death, she acknowledges as right, unable to endure the sin, though innocently committed,[127] of being known by more than one man.[128] Merely the removal from India to Lydia in marriage has signified a threat to her harmony of soul, because Kandaules, the rationalist, has been unable to muster up the proper reverence for the tradition in which she was nurtured and has tried to make her lay aside the veil,[129] but she has, until the moment of self-estrangement, maintained herself in an integral relation with herself and with her tradition.[130] This integral relation, which has hitherto constituted her life, is broken by Kandaules' introduction of Gyges into the bed-chamber by means of the magic ring which disembodies the wearer. By a twist of the ring Gyges makes himself momentarily visible to Rhodope, who is thenceforth no longer at one with herself and the Adversary who has allowed her to be stricken by the primal curse.[131] She feels that the mysterious breach between herself and the universal power, the sin of individuation, must be closed by her own death which she awaits from Kandaules.[132] Kandaules, trying to convince her that her fears are groundless, pushes assurance too far, revealing that Gyges is about to depart, and thus makes Rhodope surmise not only that Gyges was the intruder but also that Kandaules suspects this and wishes to shield him. Rhodope now sets out to secure expiation for the violation of the idea of ethical convention, from which she has been so far removed that she discards her veil as having lost its meaning.[133] Her actions do not take her back to a harmonious relation to the universal forces but separate her from them more and more, so that by a bitter paradox, through seeking atonement for an injury which, although done to her as a woman, strikes against all nature,[134] she grows to be less the representative and instrument of the Idea, as was Duke Ernst, and more the unique individual, exposed to peculiar dangers and temptations. The retribution she first demands is murder and has no semblance to justice or the impersonal necessity to which Ernst reluctantly bowed,[135] and she must even admit to Gyges that his nobility of spirit and his understanding of her have evoked a response,[136] so that she has now doubly fallen from grace, once as the unwitting victim of her husband's insensitivity and now through personal attraction to a man who is not her husband. To the metaphysical guilt of being so peculiarly perfect an embodiment of the ethical idea that her existence as a woman necessarily exposed her to defilement is added the personal guilt of unfaithfulness, though merely of inclination, to her husband. This double estrangement from her elemental nature leaves her only one resource: by marrying Gyges to restore the state of chastity in which she is known only by her husband,[137] and then by taking her life to atone for her unfaithfulness to Kandaules, to whom she would grant the release of oblivion while denying it to herself.[138]

Kandaules wins the right to oblivion, that is, reconciliation with the universal forces, by undergoing a tragic experience through which he is enabled to comprehend his relation to the universe, attaining the wisdom which wipes out all unjustified egotism and frees the spirit from death by anticipating it in the essentials.[139] But his fate is not as tragic as the incomprehensible estrangement of Rhodope from the Idea which sustained her or the absolute isolation of Gyges, who through one unwitting misstep encompasses the death of his dearest friend and of the only woman he can love. For them tragedy results from their simple existence as woman and as man, and has no connection with the specific tendency of their will to existence, which is, actually, in conformity with the universal principle. But for Kandaules tragedy springs from a personal will which is contrary to the universal principle, or the idea of ethical convention. Rhodope has to begin with no tragic focus, her original guilt is existential; Gyges' tragic focus lies in a heedless deviation from what he feels to be right; but Kandaules' tragic focus is an actual guilt and is connected with the specific tendency of his will to existence. His death is a conscious expiation of what he has done,[140] a knowing restoration of the harmony he has destroyed.[141]

The early scenes of the play show Kandaules as a naive rationalist, who insists upon discarding the insignia of royalty which have been venerated for half a millenium in Lydia,[142] because he wants a sword that can be brandished handily indoors[143] and a crown that fits his head and serves as a mounting for the precious stones that are found or will be found in his kingdom.[144] His reaction upon accepting the mysterious and awful ring of invisibility is to try it out,[145] as, of course, he immediately does, overhearing the conversation of discontented subjects and violating the sanctuary of Rhodope's slave-girls. He has never been able to acknowledge the symbolic meaning of Rhodope's veil,[146] and tries to induce her to appear at the games without it because it is difficult for him to have faith in a value which is not patent to everyone, susceptible of being tested, weighed, and measured.[147] He is so dependent upon testing, weighing, and measuring that it has seemed to Rhodope that he needed others' envy of his good fortune to feed the flame of his love.[148] He has the positivist's fundamental fault, lack of the capacity for reverence, which in his case becomes his tragic focus. His defiance of tradition, however, does not constitute a serious attempt to institute revolutionary changes. He does not try or threaten to tear up the paving blocks of society, but is merely unable to believe in any value beyond the actual positive worth of a thing. He is not in advance of his time, indeed, in one respect he shows himself to represent a less advanced position than Rhodope. It will be recalled that in *Herodes und Mariamne* the principle of oriental despotism with its cynical use of human beings to satisfy whim or desire is embodied in the old form of the Idea as represented by Herodes, whereas Mariamne, with her demand for the sanctity of the individual represents a new form, destined eventually to triumph. The relation of Mariamne to Herodes is closely analogous to the relation of Rhodope to Kandaules, whose action in revealing her to Gyges is consistent with the Homeric attitude toward women.[149] Nowhere in the play is there an indication that Kandaules planned any reforms comparable to the reforms which Herodes planned. Not lacking in strength or courage,[150] he seems to lack the resolution that comes from conviction,[151] so that enemies of the country are encouraged to attack in the belief that they can do so with impunity.[152] His inertia, together with his skepticism of traditional and transcendent values, does, indeed, arouse the resentment of his subjects, who wish to force him to resume his inherited emblems of authority, and Gyges' victory at the games makes him seem so ineffectual that there is some popular desire to depose him and elevate Gyges to his place.[153]

In Kandaules' situation as just outlined there is nothing which is necessarily tragic. In fact, if this were the entire picture it would have to be said that he was not sufficiently imposing in stature to be tragic and that his own comparison of himself to an insect that tried to change the world[154] would be quite just. It is even conceivable that the insect-pricks he inflicted would have passed unheeded. Kandaules' tragic experience stems not so much from his lack of reverence for the symbols of state as from his lack of reverence for the sanctity of the individual as imbedded in traditional moral faith. His positivist skepticism of transcendent values made him unable to see in Rhodope's veil anything more than a piece of material that kept her beauty and his good fortune from being apparent to everyone, made him share the guilt of so many of Hebbel's heroes and, be it said parenthetically, of Hebbel himself, to violate the sanctity of personality in a woman. Here Kandaules takes upon himself the original metaphysical guilt of sex, the primeval dualism with its attendant misunderstanding, injustice, egotistical exploitation. The right of the veil which Kandaules disregards, the conventional morality he flaunts, are the defenses of woman and of womanhood against desecration by man. Kandaules, in becoming aware of his relation to the great dualistic principle, also comes to understand the transcendent significance of convention and tradition, the conservative social values, which it was death for him to violate,[155] and he submits in full consciousness of what he has done and why his life is forfeit. He understands that by employing the ring for mere personal ends, he has challenged awesome, mystic forces,[156] and that the principle of ethical convention cannot be flaunted with impunity. The forms in which the principle is manifest may change, indeed, they must,[157] but they stand for something that exacts acknowledgment.[158] The unquestioning, unknowing adherence of the world to these forms gives it health and strength in a refreshing sleep.[159] Crowns, rusty swords, and veils are the baubles to which it clings in sleep and which Kandaules tries to take away. But the officious intruder, like an ineffectual insect, is brushed aside by the sleeping giant's careless hand.

Gyges is in every respect, save nobility of character, a trait which Kandaules, who refuses to allow Gyges to sacrifice himself,[160] also possesses, the opposite of his beloved friend. His sensitivity gives him a quick and ready sympathy for Thoas' feelings, injured by Kandaules' abrupt insistence upon appearing at the games attired in modern, functional regalia.[161] It is an empathic grasp of what another holds dear, but it does not stop there: having come into involuntary possession of the ring of invisibility, although he discovered the advantageous use to which it could be put, he wished to return it to the grave where he found it,[162] out of reverence for forces which he finds incomprehensible. Even in acquiescing to Kandaules' insistence that he use the ring to convince himself of Rhodope's peerless beauty, he shows reverence for what he does not understand, protesting that Kandaules' proposal must dishonor anyone but particularly a woman like Rhodope.[163] In the very moment of committing the deed he realizes that he has defiled a woman's soul, and he twists the ring upon his finger in order to be discovered and provoke retribution for his desecration.[164] When he meets Kandaules the following day his sense of having done wrong has, if anything, grown keener, and he urges Kandaules to accept the sacrifice of his life in expiation.[165] The fact that Gyges is quite the opposite of Kandaules is sensed by the Lydians, who are first impressed by his prowess in the traditional games of Hercules,[166] desire him to be their king,[167] and, indeed, upon Kandaules' death, acclaim him as such.[168]

In every particular and at every time save one Gyges is identified with the conservative and ethical forces as represented by the Lydian people in their spokesman Thoas and by Rhodope. At every point except one he upholds the principle of ethical convention which triumphs and survives in him. The one minor but crucial failure through which he suffers tragedy is characteristic of Hebbel's view that the individual, merely because he is such, must find himself in a critical relation to the Whole. It is not only Kandaules who is involved in the metaphysical guilt of sex, the primal principle of differentiation. Gyges has hitherto known woman only under the aspect of motherhood,[169] but his curiosity and desires are quickened by the sight of Lesbia at the games, and Kandaules feeds the fire of his imagination by describing Lesbia's beauty which is hidden by her veil.[170] Thus, although he knows that what he is about to do is wrong, his moral sense is numbed by the powerful impulse to come closer to the mystery of woman, his resistance is easily broken by Kandaules, who points out that the ring will shield them from detection. It needs but the sight of Rhodope to transform egocentric desire and curiosity into a pure love, the first concern of which is the beloved. He feels that because women had been a mystery to him, he had stretched out his hand for something he desired but crushed it, just as a boy will crush the bird he wants to stroke; so he has killed the only thing in the world that could be precious to him.[171] He suffers a tragedy as great or perhaps greater than Kandaules and Rhodope: not only does he in the moment of seeing Rhodope become ready for death, because he understands that everything life has to offer him has already passed into the possession of someone else,[172] but also, in order to try to save Rhodope's life he must challenge his dearest friend to mortal combat. But even slaying Kandaules does not save Rhodope, and Gyges is left in complete isolation. In all essentials he anticipates death fully as much as Kandaules, only for him the reconciliation with the universal powers is not so complete, since he does not gain the oblivion of death. Thus, as we have already seen in the case of Judith, Genoveva, Duke Ernst, and Rhodope, the individual who is in accord with the universal forces and through whose agency those powers triumph, is peculiarly exposed to tragedy. In *Gyges und sein Ring* each main character, whether opposed to or in the service of conservative social forces, acquiesces to his or her tragic destiny in order that these conservative social forces be upheld.

The *Nibelungen*,[173] Hebbel's last completed work, consisting of two five- act plays, *Siegfrieds Tod* and *Kriemhilds Rache*, and a one-act prologue, *Der gehörnte Siegfried*, is in this respect the antithesis of *Gyges und sein Ring*, being plainly progressive in its tendency. As he writes to Marie, Princess Wittgenstein,[174] it was his intention to show a new world emerging from a background of early Germanic and Christian elements. In fact, three years later, writing to Pastor Luck,[175] he says that his trilogy shows the triumph of Christianity over heathendom. To this end there are throughout the play allusions to a myth which Hebbel devised and put in the mouth of Dietrich von Bern in a scene which he later eliminated,[176] thereby creating an atmosphere of greater mystery. According to this myth, every thousand years there comes the possibility that a superman will be begotten, a giant who derives his colossal strength from all nature. If this happens, the dead gods will create a bride for him, who, if they marry, will produce a race that will destroy humanity. But the ordinary race of mortals has also one chance to survive through producing a rival bride: if the superman chooses the human bride the danger is averted. At such a moment in history the world, shaken to its depths, changes form: the past struggles up out of its grave, the future strives to be born, and the present strives to defend itself. Siegfried, of course, is the superman, Brunhild, the supernatural bride, and Kriemhild, her human rival. Siegfried, Brunhild, Frigga, and the ancient Norse gods represent a primordial and proto-human stage of cosmic evolution; most of the other characters, despite their nominal Christianity,[177] represent a stage of heathendom, with the absolute ethical norms of personal bravery, fealty, and particularly revenge; the chaplain, Rüdeger, and Dietrich von Bern represent the new form of the Idea or Christianity, with its ethical norms of self-control, humility, readiness to forgive.

On the level of the individual the antagonists are, first, Siegfried and Hagen, and then, Hagen and Kriemhild. Seen against the mythic background, these conflicts signify the successful self-defense of humanity against the might of dragons and dragon-killers, who cannot be distinguished one from the other,[178] and the inevitable self-destruction of a society whose highest law is vengeance. But a consideration of how the conflict is worked out makes it clear that here as elsewhere in Hebbel's drama the essential antagonism is not between man and man but between Adversary and individual. Siegfried is the instrument of one manifestation of the universal forces and Hagen, of another. Siegfried, by bathing in the dragon's blood, has made himself invulnerable and thus put himself outside the pale of humanity, for, as Hagen clearly recognizes, his supernatural powers remove from him the moral right to enter into combat with ordinary mortals,[179] who must exterminate him by fair means or foul along with other monsters.[180] Although Hagen is, indeed, resentful of the only hero he has met who can surpass him and who, moreover, shows a sovereign disdain for the courage and accomplishments of other men,[181] he knows and admits that Siegfried won his sword, his treasure, and his cap of invisibility through valor and strength.[182] These heroic deeds, particularly the bath in the dragon's blood which completes his superhuman attributes, making him invulnerable, except for a small spot between the shoulders, and also capable of understanding the language of the birds, are necessary steps in the supernatural design to bring Siegfried to Brunhild.[183] But Siegfried is not only a pawn of the ancient gods, he is also an individual, with personal preferences and desires: standing invisible at the edge of the lake of fire that died down when he brandished his sword, he sees Brunhild appear on the parapets of her castle, knows that he cannot love her, and goes away without revealing himself.[184] His purely human nobility becomes the tragic focus which lets destructive forces in upon himself and all the others. From this follows the wooing of Kriemhild, the subduing of Brunhild to Gunther's wishes (the characteristic Hebbelian primeval guilt of sex); there follows then the revelation of his deed to Kriemhild, the quarrel of the queens, Brunhild's disgrace. And now Hagen comes forward to kill the giant, whose mere existence has brought the entire society of the Burgundians to the brink of disaster. Hagen knows that no blame can accrue to Siegfried for revealing the deception practised on Brunhild,[185] but he also knows that the injury done his queen and king is mortal.[186] Volker, too, knows that revelation of the deed is merely a misfortune, but one that leaves the Burgundians only with the possibility of choosing who is to die, Brunhild or Siegfried. And so the deed is resolved upon, carried out with ruthlessness, and made known with brutality, and Hagen, whose code demands that even the suspicion of cowardice or dishonor be atoned in blood, takes upon himself the guilt of a dishonorable deed to avenge the honor of his master's house. His dishonor is rooted in honor: in exacting mortal punishment for the transgressions done against the form of society he represents, he commits the fatal excess, and provokes the chain of terrible retribution which ends only with the death of the last Burgundian and the promise of a new ethic to succeed the old. Thus the great antagonists, Siegfried, Hagen, Kriemhild, although they encompass each other's downfall and death are really defeated by the Adversary: Siegfried, the instrument of the old gods, because of his mysterious individual freedom sets going a series of causes and effects that necessarily lead from the failure of the attempt of the primordial past to come to life, to the bankruptcy of the fundamentally heathen present with its inevitable alternation of revenge and counter-revenge that can end only in self-destruction, to the emergence of the Christian future. The embodiment of pagan ferocity, Etzel, when his wife Kriemhild has been killed at the last by the ancient Hildebrand, cannot take up the burden which devolves upon him as a heathen king, to judge, condemn, avenge, empty new streams into the sea of blood that has already flowed, but turns instead to the third of the mighty trio, Siegfried, Etzel, Dietrich, who symbolize the three contending forms of the Idea,[187] and asks Dietrich, the Christian, to step into his place and carry the world further in its progress.

Approximately two years after he began work on the *Nibelungen* Hebbel started a play, *Demetrius*, which he never finished.[188] It deals with the same material that is the subject matter of the unfinished play, *Demetrius*, which Schiller was working on when he died, and, as is plainly evident from the fragments we possess, it was to deal with these materials in a profoundly conservative way. The central idea, the figure of the prince who has been brought up in ignorance of his identity, is one of Hebbel's earliest. According to a letter to Moritz Kolbenheyer[189] it goes back to his seventeenth year. Although this assertion has not been substantiated by other evidence, it does not seem unlikely, inasmuch as young people often indulge in the fantasy that they are not the natural children of their parents, a fantasy that might very well have had great emotional significance for Hebbel, who, as we know from Emil Kuh's biography and from his own letters and diaries, felt himself demeaned and denied his natural rights by the Kirchspielvogt Mohr, by whom he was employed from the time he was fourteen until he was twenty-two. The Demetrius of the prologue, tormented beyond endurance by the sense of being essentially far above his

menial position, can very well be taken as a reflection of the
young Hebbel in the service of the man whose patronage both
made his future life possible and also, at least in Hebbel's view,
brutally disregarded his personal qualities. Be this as it may,
it is certain that the theme of the unsuspecting prince was in his
mind when he was twenty-five: a diary entry for the nineteenth
of March, 1838,[190] mentions it as an excellent subject for a
comedy. Three years later, the idea has expanded a bit and the
diary entry for the twenty-first of January, 1841,[191] speaks of
the comic dilemma in which such a prince would find himself:
whatever course of action he takes will probably be wrong. Eight
years later still, in the diary entry for the tenth of February,
1849,[192] the comic aspect of the theme has disappeared and the
situation as it is essentially at the beginning of the play is outlined: a prince who has been brought up in obscurity and in
ignorance of his origin commits a murder, but just as the law is
about to exact the penalty it is revealed that he is above the law.
It can thus be seen that when Hebbel's attention was directed to
the Demetrius theme by his interest in re-working Schiller's uncompleted play, he was taking up a problem that had long had
considerable significance for him. Unfortunately, he did not
live to complete the play and, even though he did finish over four
acts in addition to the prologue it is not at all clear how the denouement would have come about. None the less, enough of the
play exists in a sufficiently finished form to allow certain conclusions as to its general tendency. The fifth act, of which two
hundred thirty lines were written, could not conceivably have
been intended to reverse and nullify everything that had preceded and therefore it would seem that the play must be admitted
in evidence and given its due weight.[193]

The background, which Hebbel considered particularly important in this play,[194] is the Slavic domains of Russia and Poland
at the time of the usurper Boris Godunow,[195] who is a minor
character in the play and is given very sympathetic treatment.
Demetrius is the son of the late Czar Ivan the Terrible and a
palace-servant, born at the same time as a legitimate son of Ivan
and Marfa Nagoy. The Jesuits, in order to install a czar who
will open the Russian Empire to the Roman Church, believe they
have persuaded the palace-servant Barbara to steal the new-born

prince, leaving her own son, of whose paternity they are ignorant, in place of the legitimate heir. Barbara, however, deceives the Jesuits and turns over to them her own son, who she can truthfully swear is the child of Ivan. The true prince is killed and thus with Ivan, who has murdered another son with his own hands, comes to an end the line of Russian rulers whose legitimate descent from Rurik constitutes their absolute right to the throne. The illegitimate son of Ivan, Demetrius, has grown up in Poland as a kind of half menial, half foster-child, of Mniczek, the woiwod or governor of Sendomir. He has a natural majesty, an inborn power to command respect and obedience, an overwhelming sense of having nothing in common with the other servants of the household and of being superior even to his master and the Polish nobles, who are Mniczek's associates. His impossible position is especially poignant because he is in love with Mniczek's daughter Marina, who is socially so far above him that his love is both hopeless and inordinately presumptuous. When the play opens with the prologue the pressure of resentment against the fact that every natural expression of his personality is illegitimate has reached the point where a violent explosion can be set off by almost any incident. This incident is provoked by the attempt of the nobleman Odowalski to rebuke and chastise him for being too familiar with Marina. Demetrius challenges Odowalski to a duel, a challenge which Odowalski quite naturally ignores, since Demetrius is not a gentleman. Demetrius then rushes upon the defenseless Odowalski and murders him without compunction. Although committed in fury this act is not blind or senseless, but is instead a kind of attempt at suicide.[196] As such it fails because the monk Gregory and the Cardinal-Legate come forward with the announcement that Demetrius is the legitimate heir to the throne of Russia and therefore above the law, an announcement which gives Demetrius for the first time the right to be his true self.[197] This is a right, however, which he has gained through committing a murder, which has as its most profound motive to challenge the social order to do away with him. The whole prologue serves as the setting for this murder, which puts into motion the tragic forces that have been poised for years. No more forceful dramatic emphasis could be given to the fact that Demetrius achieves self-realization through violent transgression and personal guilt. Not even his subsequent scrupulous regard for law, the popular welfare, and the principle of legitimacy can efface this.

The principle of legitimacy is conceived as the absolute standard of this time and place: although the Russian nobles may conceal their personal motives under the cloak of allegiance to the principle,[198] none the less, the principle is so absolute that the fate of two monarchs and their followers as well as the fate of the realm depends upon it. When Demetrius repeatedly risks his life from a feeling that he must not allow even the suspicion to rest upon him that he has less personal bravery than any soldier who fights for him, Mniczek points out that he must not suppose that nameless thousands are ready to sacrifice their lives for him as an individual. Their sacrifice is offered to the principle of imperial majesty, which he represents, and which has had from the beginning of time the right to let loose the powers of hell in order to subdue its foes. For just as certainly as the power of majesty alone has subdued diabolical powers, just as certainly does it have the right to unleash them in its defense when it is threatened.[199] The right of a legitimate son of Ivan to assemble an army to depose Boris is universally accepted. The cardinal-legate counted upon this when he planned to have Ivan's son brought up outside Russia so as to use him as a tool to open the Russian Empire to the Roman Church and he is certain that all the peoples of Russia will gather around the battle-flags of the true heir.[200] In fact, Boris himself, who had by no means been eager to claim the throne, says he would turn over his imperial sway to Demetrius if he could believe his claim to be valid.[201] Demetrius himself does believe it to be valid, partly because of the evidence of Gregory and the cardinal-legate but more because royal ancestry would explain to him the otherwise mysterious feeling of superiority which had given him so much torment because he had no right to it. Having suffered beyond endurance because of illegitimacy, he prizes legitimacy so much more, and by his very first decisions, to make no significant social changes within the empire without the advice of his legal counsellors,[202] prepares us for a decision to renounce his claim and even life itself when he learns that, even though he is Ivan's son, he is not the rightful prince because his mother was not the czarina: for him his claim is valid only as long as it is legitimate.[203]

From what has been said so far it might seem as though Hebbel's characteristic feeling that tragedy is inherent in the relationship of the significant individual to the Whole is absent from *Demetrius*: the exciting cause of the tragedy is a crime committed by the hero. And it is true that real personal guilt contributes a great deal to the tragic experience of the two characters who are the central tragic figures: Demetrius and his supposed mother Marfa. None the less, for both of them, tragedy comes because their actions, springing from what they are, constitute the fatal excess. Any action on their part must lead to doom and the only possibility of avoiding it lies in taking no action whatever, that is, surrender and negation of self. Marfa, the widow of Czar Ivan, has gone into involuntary retirement in a cloister[204] but has become reconciled to her life there and has, in fact, nearly attained the degree of self-abnegation which brings reconciliation with the Idea by anticipating death in the essentials,[205] desiring to live longer only to complete her purification and the atonement of her great wrong-doing.[206] She has been broken by contrition for the terrible vengeance which she visited on the guilty and the innocent alike for the death of her child.[207] Her tragic focus lay in the fact of being the czarina, for the crown doubles the power of the demons that tempt, and halves the power of the angels that warn: had she been no different from other mothers, she would at most have killed herself.[208] This woman is once more and against her will made to participate in affairs of state: Hiob, the patriarch, wishes her to go to Moscow to pray at the tomb of the murdered child, thus giving evidence that the real Demetrius is dead, but Otrepiep, the unprincipled and despicable adventurer, takes her to Demetrius' camp in order to reap a reward for having strengthened the latter's claims. She goes to Demetrius, hoping for a sign, for positive intuitional knowledge whether he is her son or not, but the sign for which she has implored heaven is not given. Demetrius' resemblance to Ivan makes her think that he must be her son, but she has no certainty. But, having no inner conviction that Demetrius is an impostor, she does not denounce him and thereby even aids him, for her apparent acceptance of him gives widespread credence to his claim and gains him many followers. Marfa, unable to endure the heavy responsibility of being the cause of so many warriors perishing in the struggle with Boris seeks certainty at the tomb of the child in Moscow. But meanwhile she has been deeply moved by Demetrius' nobility and goodness so that the wish that he might be the true prince suppresses her inner voice until the moment when Mniczek, for political reasons, orders the removal of the casket from the royal tomb. Then, within hearing of the assembled citizens of Moscow she cries "No!" and the abbess, who has been her companion, knows that she has obtained intuitional certainty.[209] Coming thus publicly, her knowledge must have the most serious consequences for Demetrius, for the people are very readily swayed by rumors and reports, and this time they see an action which can have only one meaning: that the new czar is an impostor. Marfa, convinced of Demetrius' nobility of character, tries to counteract what has happened by bestowing a public blessing upon Demetrius, but she cannot bless him as being the rightful heir, but only as deserving happiness because of his greatness and nobility. These scenes constitute the climax of the play: at this point it becomes clear to the spectators that Demetrius' claim is false, and the rest of the play must set forth how the truth is revealed to Demetrius (the magnificent fourth act) and how he meets his fate. Marfa, by emerging from the half-death of the cloister and once more taking part in the great events of history, merely by virtue of being what she is, the czarina, loses the hard-won and precarious tranquillity that was almost within her grasp and, contrary to her will, helps bring about the defeat and death of the only human being who commands her love and respect, the false Demetrius.

Demetrius' tragic focus, the slaying of Odowalski, constitutes real personal guilt, but in a deeper sense this guilt is existential. The entry in Hebbel's diary will be recalled in which he wrote of the dilemma of the unsuspecting prince: whatever course of action he takes will be wrong. Demetrius, like every individual in Hebbel's view, is by nature illegitimate. In the prologue the conflict between his real and apparent nature has reached such a pitch of intensity that he longs for death and, as we have seen, murders Odowalski as a challenge to the society which has had no place for him. He is so absolute an individual that, unable to endure the restraint put upon him by society, he prefers death to life, but, in seeking death, does what he can to strike at the universal forces which deny him the right to be himself. If he could have avoided guilt, it would have been through the sacrifice of his essential self. However, he asserts himself and through his self-assertion seems to gain the possibility and the right to live. But his new life is just as illegitimate as the old and is doomed to failure, no matter what he does: Marfa's perception of the unwitting imposture must be fatal in any case. Demetrius, however, who has shown by every action since the revelation of his supposed descent, that he reveres established tradition and believes without reservation in the principle of legitimacy, will not fall an unwilling victim to the absolute forces. His greatest temptation comes just after Gregory reveals that he has the backing of the Roman Church, which has secreted him in order to secure acknowledgment in Russia through him. This means that Demetrius has the support of the Roman Church and the possibility of closing the ecclesiastical schism. Demetrius' reply is that he will never interfere with the divine order of things and, after Gregory has gone, that his people must be free to worship as they choose, decisions which he does not revoke when he learns from Marfa that he is only an illegitimate son of Ivan. It does not even occur to Demetrius to seek his allies where he can find them: his first impulse is to call the nobles together, reveal the truth, and seek their leave to return to Poland where the executioner will be waiting for him. Mniczek, however, is quick to point out that Demetrius cannot hope to avoid further guilt through this course of action either, for if he gives up now he will necessarily plunge Mniczek, Marina and all his other loyal followers to destruction. Demetrius understands this and thus resolves to impersonate the czar, sacrifice his peace of mind and conscience, until he can provide for the safety of his friends and then encompass his own destruction.[210] The individual seeks tragic reconciliation with the absolute forces and dies in order to uphold them. *Demetrius* is uncompromisingly conservative.

PART THREE

Mystic Formulations: Religio-Poetic Expression

PART THREE

MYSTIC FORMULATIONS: RELIGIO-POETIC EXPRESSION

"Ein Atmen über mir, als ob's mich einziehen will.—Alles Leben ist Raub des Einen am Anderen." Hebbel, Tagebücher, 12. März 1841.

"Du atmest fremden Tod als Dein Leben ein und fremdes Leben als Deinen Tod aus." Hebbel, Tagebücher, 20. März 1857.

"In dem Augenblick, wo das Elixier des ewigen Lebens entdeckt wird, können die Menschen nicht mehr zeugen—der Brunnen trocknet aus. Es stirbt Niemand mehr, es wird aber auch Niemand mehr geboren." Hebbel, Tagebücher, 31. Mai 1844.

It will be recalled how Hebbel's attitude toward the question of social change as revealed in his diaries, letters, and poems tended at one time to be progressive and at another to be conservative, alternating in an irregular rhythm between these two poles. And the same kind of alternation has been revealed in the plays. But whether he saw the cosmic process as an upward movement or as a mere oscillation, he saw it at all times as a flux, a never ceasing interaction of opposed forces, all life being the struggle of the individual against the Absolute. From the relatively early diary entry[1] to the effect that the individual, eternally in the process of being created, prevents the universe from terminating in rigidity to the very late one[2] to the effect that nature has made the total life process dependent upon the metabolic flow of individuals, just as the individual life process is dependent upon the metabolic flow of basic substances, this notion of compact flux persists without fundamental change. For Hebbel this means that nothing essentially new can enter the universe, which must be a kind of closed system, but only that often an element disappears at one place to reappear at another.[3] The process is like the melting of an icicle: the water drips down and re-forms into ice below.[4] Discovery of an elixir of life would be like a sudden freeze that prevented the upper icicle from dropping away: at the moment when an elixir of life should be discovered, human beings would no longer be able to beget children, no one would die but no one would be born.[5] The process of compact flux is in such perfect balance that no one can be born unless someone else has previously just died:[6] you breathe in another's death as your life and you breathe out your own death as another's life.[7]

Hebbel's conception of the world has often been called a dualism and, indeed, he himself accepted dualism as the basic and ultimate principle: it dominates all our ideas and thoughts, making it possible for us to conceive of life and death, health and disease, time and eternity, but not to comprehend any unifying and reconciling principle that is the ground of these antagonisms.[8] He recognizes that Schelling's conception that at a certain time God the Son of necessity proceeded from God the Father projects the fundamental dualism into the Deity, and makes God the root of the cosmic disunity.[9] Humanity is irrevocably divided against itself by the primeval dualism, of which Jewry and heathendom in *Judith* are only representatives.[10] Fundamentally, the cosmic process seems to be one of complete estrangement to the point of hostility and then a self-reconciliation through love.[11] Hate and love would therefore be designations of opposite universal tendencies: individuation involves its own punishment, so that universal hate has replaced universal love, which ought to prevail.[12] But if it is true that universal love ought to prevail and that the cosmic process leads to a reconciliation through love, a single absolute principle seems to be implied, rather than two co-equal and opposed principles, which would seem necessary for a consistent dualism. And, indeed, Hebbel does speak of the aboriginal feeling of existence, higher than the tension of love and hate, a feeling with which God embraces the world.[13] This leads to the conception of an all inclusive Absolute or Whole, a differentiated monistic Absolute in compact flux, the dualism consisting in the mysterious differentiation and freedom of the individual from the Whole, or God. The antagonists in Hebbel's dualism are not the Devil and God, but man and God, who is the Adversary.

"Man conceived his own opposite and he had his God."[14] This is one of a considerable number of Hebbel's groping attempts to formulate his feeling about God. Another one is: "God is everything, because he is nothing, nothing finite."[15] This pantheistic conception is very early in Hebbel: in July 1835 he notes in his diary[16] that God is the essence of all power, physical as well as spiritual, even having sensual desires. Or again he conceives of God as an all-pervasive atmosphere in which the mind breathes and has its being just as the body has its being in the air, so that every thought and every feeling is a breath of God.[17] Or God is the self-consciousness of the world, analogous to the self-consciousness of the individual; whether He exists or not, none can say, but it is certain that if He does not exist the world has no purpose.[18] All manifestations of the finite are an irridescence of the One and Everlasting,[19] and the world is a great wound inflicted upon God.[20] The last figure occurs in a good many variations, being one of Hebbel's favorite metaphors for the relation of the individual to the Whole. For example, he writes that it would not be impossible that man's consciousness as an individual is a feeling of pain in the same sense that a finger or some other member of the body becomes, so to speak, self-conscious, when it is injured and no longer has its normal relation to the whole organism.[21] The elegiac distichs entitled "Das Urgeheimnis"[22] rephrase this idea: "How does pain originate? Just as life does. If your finger hurts you, this means that the finger has been dissociated from the body and the juices are beginning to circulate in it independently. Thus the individual is only a pain in God." And the yearning for immortality is the smart of the wound that was caused when the individuals were torn away from the Whole, to begin separate existence, like the dissevered members of a polyp.[23] At this point it begins to be plain that if, in Hebbel's view, God is the self-consciousness of the world and if the individual becomes aware only through the pain of separation from the Whole, there is an interdependence of individual and Absolute: the finite being is necessary for the liberation and self-realization of the Infinite Being or, as we have seen (p.73, above) the ceaseless emergence of individual forms prevents the Absolute from terminating in rigidity. At the same time, the individual forms, being finite, prevent a complete and perfect realization of the Absolute: the Deity is corseted by the created world[24] and man is the Procrustes-bed of God.[25] Therefore every process of thought is an effort of God to find Himself, that would succeed much sooner if He did not also seek to lose Himself;[26] that is, the Absolute can be realized, although imperfectly, only in the individual forms, whose ultimate and highest destiny is to be reunited through submergence with the Absolute. Finite and infinite are interdependent: the Eternal must dream about the Temporal, just as the Temporal dreams about the Eternal.[27]

This interdependence goes so far that it occurs to Hebbel as a strange possibility that God may not have given birth to the world but the world to God.[28] In the world a God lies buried, who seeks to be resurrected, to break through at every point, in love and in every noble deed.[29] Therefore, if God the Creator does not exist, God the Creature is at least conceivable: if there is not a colossal Individual in the beginning, why not at the end?[30] But these speculations are only extremely bold formulations of the basic interdependence of God and the world. Hebbel's usual and more sober belief postulated God as the originally undifferentiated Whole, the greatest single Being, a sort of counterbalance to the individual beings, into which it is constantly breaking up.[31] However, as he wrote to Pastor Luck,[32] on the standpoint which the pastor represented there is certainty of a personal God and of immortality, but on Hebbel's own standpoint everything is a mystery and every attempt to solve the riddle of the universe is a tragedy of thought.

But whatever the ultimate nature of the mystery, in Hebbel's view the basic concept is an Absolute which, through the principle of individuation, consists of a myriad individual forms, whose existence depends upon the Absolute but whose existence is just as necessary to the Absolute, which, but for them, must terminate in a static rigidity.[33] As we know, a constant flux, an unceasing metabolic flow of individuals is necessary to bring life into this kind of universe, and it is on this basis that there is some justification for considering Hebbel's concept of the universe dualistic. However this may be, it is a concept which must spring from a particular sense of existence, a specific *Lebensgefühl*. The pertinent passages in Hebbel's diaries and letters reveal a rather consistent intuitional and emotional orientation to questions of metaphysical import from early to late in life.

To turn now from the monistic differentiated Absolute under the aspect of the Whole, to the same Absolute under the aspect of the individual, we find there that the flux which gives life to the Whole means death to the individual forms, the disappearance of one form being necessary for the emergence of another. Therefore, in Hebbel's view, to know what life is one must ask what death is,[34] for life is only a different death, the birth of life and not its end,[35] a mask which life assumes.[36] Life is the attempt of the recalcitrant individual to free itself from the Whole and exist independently, but the attempt can succeed only as long as the force lasts which the individual has taken from the Whole,[37] and therefore the individual must sink back into the undifferentiated Whole when this force is exhausted. But the individual does not merely sink back, as into repose, but it is constantly assailed by the universal forces.[38] Diminution in the power of an individual form opens an opportunity for other forms to attack and replace it: you breathe in another's death as your own life and you breath out another's life as your own death.[39] Small wonder that Hebbel at times felt that the history of mankind was like the dream of a beast of prey.[40]

Viewed from the perspective of the Absolute, the compact flux is life; viewed from the perspective of the individual, the flux is neither life nor death, but the two together, a death-life. There is only death and there is no death, for even decay is only a disintegration of complex life into independent atomistic parts.[41] But, whereas the process may be death-life, the individual must die in order for the process to be carried on. Life and death are so inextricably intertwined that there is probably not a speck of dust on the whole earth that has not at one time been alive, laughing, weeping, blossoming with fragrance,[42] and in every atom of each of us there is already developing a flower or an animal, which can, of course, come to life only through our death; immortality of the individual could thus be achieved through the utterance of some magic word that would kill these unformed lives.[43] Although, to be sure, Hebbel calls this last notion fantastic, it none the less fits in consistently with his serious attempts to grapple with first and last things, and with the thought we have already quoted (p. 73, above) that the discovery of the elixir of life would bring all procreation to a stand-still through a petrifaction of the process of death-life. Among the earliest entries in his diaries there are several which deal with the possibility of using the discovery of the elixir of life as the theme of a *Novelle*: since the discovery would mean that the dead could never live again, the situation of a man who discovered it after the loss of his beloved would be particularly poignant and suitable.[44] This last speculation seems to imply that Hebbel believed in personal immortality and, indeed, he does seem to have held such a belief, at least, for some time, although he seems also not to have been very seriously concerned with this question,[45] and his speculations about it do not follow the clear line that is discernible in his feeling about the nature of God and the universe.[46] For example, he has great hesitation to maintain that the individual soul has always been, and feels that only on this assumption can the future immortality of the soul be postulated,[47] and seems also to feel that continuation of conscious personal existence into infinite time is scarcely conceivable, but that unending existence without consciousness is quite possible.[48] But regardless of the mortality or immortality of the individual soul, the finite individual is, as we have seen, involved in a never ending process of generation through annihilation. The finest symbol of life is the fly that dies in copulation: its whole existence has been merely a preparation for the supreme moment and at this moment comes disintegration after the spark of life has been passed on to a new creature, and so there is an unending chain that constantly leads up to the point of gratification but never beyond it.[49] Or another symbol is the lizard which snaps up a fly and at the same instant is devoured by an adder.[50]

From what has just preceded it would seem to be apparent that Hebbel's *Weltanschauung* is not so much an intellectually conceived and rationally developed system as it is an immediate and intuitional or experiential reaction to life. In the attempt to make his *Weltanschauung* articulate he did undoubtedly use terms and concepts that stem from Hegel and Schelling among others,[51] but this circumstance ought not to obscure the fact that the ideas which have been discussed here, for example, those which have been called the idea of death-life, or the compact flux, were lived by Hebbel and not collected from outside sources. They visited him in his dreams and were the projection of an almost corporeal *Lebensgefühl*. On the sixth of July, 1837, he notes this dream in his diary:[52]

> Last night I dreamt I saw old king Maximilian Joseph buried and King Ludwig crowned. Both events took place in the burial vault and the funeral rites were dreadfully intermingled with the coronation ceremony: the funerary torches did duty in the procession at the coronation, and when King Ludwig donned the crown King Maximilian nodded his head from out of his coffin. I was among the coronation officials; when we came up again King

Ludwig locked the vault and said, giving me the key: Don't let him out, but don't let me in either!

At another time[53] he writes of having a sense of something breathing above him as though it wanted to suck him in and he adds that every life is lived at the expense of another. Or again he writes:[54]

> As soon as a man becomes conscious of himself and stands erect, he feels something like a pressure from above, and yet he is alive only insofar as he is conscious of himself. It is as if he were emerging from an abyss and were always being pushed back again by an unknown hand.

As can be expected, this basic sense of life finds expression, often very powerful expression, in Hebbel's lyric poetry, assuming various guises but never fundamentally changing from the earliest years to the latest.

Hebbel apparently thought his conception of the world as containing the individual forms just as the ocean contains the drops of water which constitute it so profound and significant an idea that it could comfort Elise Lensing for the death of their child.[55] While acknowledging ignorance of the ultimate cause of the separation of the individual from the matrix of the Whole, suggesting that it might be to channel off and break up the force of evil or that only through this process could the Deity gain self-consciousness, he professes the belief that the individuals can gain certainty on this point only through death, through merging with the Whole like drops of water that roll along in the ocean wave. This, of course, is the conception of the all-inclusive but differentiated Absolute which has already been described (p. 74, above), a world that is so full that it would be rigid save for the principle of individuation, by which, in constant flow, one being replaces another. The constant flow is pictured also in "Requiem,"[56] a poem in which the souls of the dead are conceived as hovering near the survivors who held their memory dear until loving memory fails; then the storm of the night seizes them and whirls them away through unending desolation where life ceases to be, where there is only a struggle of unleashed forces for renewed existence. The thought of disembodied spirits pushing each other, and, by inference, incarnate beings also, out of the way in a struggle to gain material existence is a vivid and terrifying one, and one that recurs in different guise in a good many poems, as will be seen. But not only do the disembodied individuals strive to return to life, but the living and finite beings can transcend their limits, at least for brief moments, and harbour the spirit of the universe.[57] Then the individual has a brief glimpse into the dark rifts of the Unknown and has a direct intuition of the world. In another poem,[58] however, in which Hebbel wishes he were able to unwind the thread that leads into the center of the cosmic riddle and see how the Whole and the One are merged into each other, he expresses the fear that such an attempt, if successful, would annihilate him: just as he has suppressed thoughts which threatened his existence, he fears that the Absolute would in self-defense suppress an ego that threatened to penetrate too far. None the less, it is the right and the nature of the individual to call pain and grief down upon itself in its defiance of hostile universal forces.[59] If it is strong enough in its challenge and defiance the gods will refuse nothing except knowledge of the ultimate secret, the primeval source of light. This, the individual *should* seek to attain, knowing that the attainment will destroy him and merge him with the Infinite. In fact, according to another poem,[60] the yearning to be merged with the Infinite is the only real content of crepuscular earthly existence.

Thus, the finite and the Infinite, the earthly and the unearthly, life and death, are inextricably interwoven in the poet's feelings, in his personal sense of death-life. As an instance we may take the poem "Geburtsnacht-Traum,"[61] which describes a dream in which he saw all his ancestors assembled at his side and they seemed to take a profound interest in him. It was the hour which saw his birth and now he must ask himself in trembling whether life and death continue to be intertwined even in the grave. This is the same kind of feeling that is expressed in "Nachtgefühl,"[62] a poem in which he thinks of the time when his mother undressed him for the night and of the time when his neighbors will undress him for burial; when he goes to sleep he often dreams of one time or the other, but cannot be sure which is which. A very early expression of the feeling occurs in "Der Zauberer,"[63] which tells in ballad form an anecdote similar to the story of Hartmann von Aue's *Der arme Heinrich*: In order to save her beloved from death a girl allows a "wise man" to cut open her heart to obtain the healing blood which brings her lover back from death. But when, upon recovery, the man hears that the girl has died, he closes his eyes once more in eternal sleep. Although the ending makes the poem an imperfect and deviant expression of the theme of interlocking life and death, the sense of death-life is central to the anecdote, inasmuch as the life of the one is dependent upon the death of the other. In "Die junge Mutter,"[64] a young woman who has just born a child dies very soon after the death of the baby; Hebbel's observation is: the angel of death came forth from her womb. The significance, of course, lies in the fact that the angel of death came forth from the source of life. The death of the mother through the child is a special form of a theme that may be called the violent and hostile succession of generations, another guise of the sense of compact flux. It is connected with the dream already mentioned above (p. 78, above) of the intermingling funeral and coronation of the two kings. It occurs in various forms in the poems. For example,[65] the reigning king walks past the vault where his father, whom he dethroned, lies buried. A voice from the vault calls out that he has come a whole day too early. Shuddering, the king returns to his palace to learn that his son is planning to usurp the royal power by force the following day. The king then summons his son and invests him with the regalia of kingship, hoping thus to redress the balance, for as he says, God has promised him to do unto him as he does unto others. Or, in another variant,[66] the robber captain commands a young recruit to commit a murder in order to wean him away from God, saying that he had taken the step himself by killing his own father. Thereupon the recruit stabs the robber captain to death. Another variant[67] has a more conciliatory ending. An old man has lifted his little grandson up to the straw roof of his son's house so that the child could put a candle to it. The son, in a fury, attacks his father and drags him to an abyss into which he wishes to hurl him. The old man begs not to be thrown into the depths because he himself hurled his own father over the edge at that very spot and he is sure that his spirit will never find peace there. By this time the little boy has caught up with the two men, and the father, seeing him and foreseeing the endless chain of violence that he is about to continue resolves to break it off and vows to cherish his father no matter what he may do.

The notion of compact flux is connected in Hebbel's sense of life with a feeling of being threatened by hostile forces on every hand, of being pushed out of life. It was a feeling which he knew very well from his own home, where there were so many mouths to feed and just so much to feed them with. Each member of the household could assert itself only at the expense of the others: the family dog, which the boy Hebbel loved dearly, had to be killed because it required too much to eat. Hebbel's father even, according to the diaries,[68] resented the appetite of his growing sons:

> My father really hated me and we could not love him, either. A slave of marriage, bound to poverty with iron fetters, chained to bare necessity, and, in spite of the exertion of all his strength and of his extreme effort, unable to advance even so much as a single step, he hated happiness. The approach to his heart was blocked by thistles and thorns, and he could not endure happiness in the faces of his own children. Joyous laughter that expands the bosom was a grave wrong, mockery directed against him. . . . He called my brother and me his wolves; our appetite took his away. We could only rarely eat a slice of bread without having to hear that we didn't deserve it.

The sense of being hemmed in on all sides and of being elbowed out of his *Lebensraum* did not leave him when he entered the service of Kirchspielvogt Mohr: there he was cut off by the very thin but rigid line of social class from association with people whose intellectual stature was comparable to his own, having to eat with the menial servants and share a narrow cot with the coachman even through an illness of the latter. The sense of hostile forces bearing in upon him was something that he experienced both in mind and body and left a very deep mark upon him: it took him very long to overcome the sense of oppression in a social gathering, and even when he had gained general recognition his long rankling sense of social inferiority found such amusing and rather ludicrous expressions as the famous calling-cards engraved with the title: *Chevalier de plusieurs ordres*.

The sense of being pushed out of life finds direct personal expression in a number of lyric poems. In "Dämmer-Empfindung"[69] he wonders what it is that drives him away from here and mysteriously pulls him into some other place; and he speculates whether it can be some incorporeal spirit that is crowding him into death in order to gain life for itself as his heir, or, whether, perhaps, in the beyond the grapes have ripened which are waiting to be plucked by his hand. In "Das Grab"[70] he speaks of a feeling that impelled him to dig a grave, even though it was much against his will to do so, and when he had finished, his arms sank to his sides in exhaustion and his only wish was to lie down in the grave he had just dug. In another poem[71] the universal hostility of life to life is objectified in a picture which is reminiscent of the diary entry which finds a symbol of life in the lizard being devoured by an adder as it snaps up a fly (p.78): over the desert a vulture hovers searching for prey; below in the sand a weary pilgrim plods along; the one is on the point of starving to death and the other, on the point of dying of thirst; when the two see each other they are eager to meet because each longs for the flesh or blood of the other. Another poem[72] recalls the diary entry which saw in the fly that dies in copulation the highest symbol of life (above, p. 78), but in the poem the same basic conception is presented as a powerful, terrifying, and exultant personal experience. It is a stormy night and the wind is ruffling and tearing the leaves from the trees while the poet embraces his beloved. His caresses pull a rose-bud out of her hair; it falls at her feet and, a goddess of death, she tramples it into the dust as her response to his embrace grows more fervent, and the wind carries off the scarf with which she has always covered her throat and bosom. At the height of his ardor the poet cries out that he and his beloved sense time rushing past with the speed of the wind and dare to surrender to their desires: before him is the allurement of her full and fiery lips, two steps behind him, brandishing his scythe, is death. The same basic feeling is just as beautifully expressed in one of the early poems, "Nachtlied."[73] The poet tells his awe of the surging and pulsating night, full of flaming stars in the everlasting reaches where some dreadful power has been aroused; his heart is contracted within his bosom as he feels the colossal stirring of the life force in the ebb and flow that threatens to snuff out his own life. But then sleep approaches him as the nurse approaches a child and draws the protective magic circle around his feeble flickering flame.

The bearing of the immediately foregoing discussion of the lyric poems which have been considered upon the question of Hebbel's conception of social progress would seem to be rather clear. The irregularly rhythmic oscillation of Hebbel's expressed beliefs, insights, and convictions between the poles of progressivism and conservatism has been traced in his diaries and letters. A similar oscillation, though one that is necessarily not parallel in time to the brief notations of the diaries and letters, has been shown to exist in the plays. The opposite poles of progressivism and conservatism are so clearly contradictory and mutually exclusive that it sometimes seems difficult to understand how so self-conscious a writer as Hebbel could be so inconsistent. The present study has revealed that there is good reason to believe that this undeniable inconsistency springs from a source deep within Hebbel's psychic experience and that the fundamental problem is not so well expressed in terms of social and historical progress as it is in terms of a metaphysical conception of a universal compact flux through a process of death-life. The notion of the compact flux can be taken as a necessary consequence of the dualism, Absolute and Individual, Whole and Part: The Whole breaks up into a myriad transient forms. If it is the *Whole* which breaks up, there is no *space* between these forms, but only *time*. Therefore a form can exist only in a space which once was occupied by another form. Therefore the number of simultaneous individuals is always at a maximum and the only movement that takes place must be a movement of succession, not necessarily to a higher level of existence, though that may be the case in specific instances, but always to a stage of renewed dynamic equilibrium. There is only one supreme law: that the Whole be maintained; the individual is of no consequence; if the existence of the individual form upsets the equilibrium it must be punished, that is, eliminated; but there is no reason whatever why it should be compensated for any misfortune that befalls it.

The sense of life which has just been summarized in terms that seek to convey on the level of conceptual understanding what really does not belong on this level at all, is, one can say with some assurance, a primàl experience, personal, religio-poetic, even almost corporeal in its immediacy. Its nature is mystical, not syllogistic or dialectic. It is almost ineffable, undergoing a multitude of only nearly and almost wholly articulate formulations in the diaries and letters, and in the plays and poems. There is no rigid consistency of formulation, there cannot be, since what is formulated is a psychic state, not a logical conclusion.[74] Fundamentally, Hebbel's plays are not the allegorical garments of a philosophy of history, but moving images of life as caught and recorded in the camera obscura of a poet's soul.

NOTES

PART ONE

1 Cf. Anna Schapire-Neurath, *Friedrich Hebbel* (Leipzig, 1909); Oskar Walzel, *Hebbelprobleme* (Leipzig, 1909); id., *Friedrich Hebbel und seine Dramen* (Leipzig, Berlin, 1927), pp.120ff.; Hans M. Wolff, "Die Doppelstellung Herzog Albrechts in Hebbels *Agnes Bernauer*," *MFDU*, XXXI, pp.209ff.; Ludwig Marcuse, "Der Hegelianer Friedrich Hebbel—gegen Hegel," *MFDU*, XXXIX,pp.506ff.
2 Cf. Paul G. Graham, *The Relation of History to Drama in the Works of Friedrich Hebbel* (Smith College Studies in Modern Languages, XV, Nos.1-2, Northampton, 1933-34), 5-7.
3 Friedrich Hebbel, "Wandlung," *Sämtliche Werke, Historisch-Kritische Ausgabe* (R. M. Werner, ed., Berlin, 1904-1907), VII, 57. This edition will be cited as follows: Part I, *Werke* as *Wke.*; Part II, *Tagebücher* as *Tgb.*; Part III, *Briefe* as *Br.*
4 "Der Mensch" (1833), *Wke.*, VII, 107.
5 *Wke.*, VII, 126 (1835).
6 "Das alte Haus" (25 June 1834), *Wke.*, VI, 266.
7 *Br.*, I, 136-137, # 38, 19 Dec. 1836.
8 *Br.*, I, 140-141, # 40, 30 Dec. 1836.
9 *Br.*, I, 141-142, # 41, 7 Jan. 1837.
10 *Br.*, I, 163, # 43, 12 Febr. 1837, to Elise Lensing.
11 *Tgb.*, I, 249, # 1167, 4 June 1838.
12 *Br.*, I, 323, # 78, 30 Sept. 1838, to Elise Lensing.
13 *Tgb.*, I, 286, # 1340, 24 Nov. 1838.
14 *Tgb.*, I, 294, # 1363, 28 Nov. 1838.
15 *Tgb.*, I, 294-295, # 1364, 28 Nov. 1838.
16 *Tgb.*, I, 295, # 1367, 28 Nov. 1838.
17 *Tgb.*, I, 12, # 45, 11 July 1835.
18 "Lebensmomente" (1836), *Wke.*, VII, 142.
19 *Br.*, I, 194-195, # 48, 11 April 1837, to Elise Lensing.
20 *Tgb.*, I, 216-217, # 1011, 6 March 1838.
21 *Tgb.*, I, 256, # 1206, 21 June 1838.
22 *Tgb.*, I, 286, # 1337, 24 Nov. 1838.
23 *Tgb.*, I, 292, # 1356, 27 Nov. 1838.
24 It is customary, and, in a certain sense, fitting, to distinguish only two main periods in Hebbel's development, as, to mention one of the most recent extensive discussions of Hebbel as a dramatist, von Wiese does in *Die deutsche Tragödie von Lessing bis Hebbel*. Indeed, Hebbel himself recognized that he had reached such a turning point, writing to Rötscher on the 22nd of December, 1847 (*Br.*, IV, 71, # 256) that *Julia* is a product of his transition from an old sphere of existence to a new one. Nonetheless, it is possible to discern within the first period, before his marriage, an earlier, more generally progressive phase, and a later phase of sharp fluctuation. Cf. Benno von Wiese,

Die deutsche Tragödie von Lessing bis Hebbel (Hamburg, 1948), II, 378-461.
25 *Tgb.*, I, 306, # 1418, 6 Jan. 1839.
26 *Tgb.*, I, 317-318, # 1471, 2 Febr. 1839.
27 *Tgb.*, II, 38-39, # 1989, 23 April 1840.
28 *Tgb.*, II, 41-42, # 1995, 26 April 1840.
29 *Tgb.*, II, 44, # 2005, 28 April 1840.
30 *Tgb.*, II, 47, # 2025, 20 May 1840.
31 *Tgb.*, II, 55, # 2064, 27 July 1840.
32 *Tgb.*, II, 111, # 2235, 29 April 1841.
33 "Die menschliche Gesellschaft," *Wke.*, VI, 316.
34 "Der Mensch und die Geschichte," *Wke.*, VI, 320.
35 "Unsere Zeit," *Wke.*, VI, 315, 4 Sept. 1841.
36 *Tgb.*, II, 137, # 2437, 12 Jan. 1842.
37 "Das höchste Gesetz," *Wke.*, VII, 186, spring 1842.
38 *Tgb.*, II, 178, # 2550, 13 May 1842.
39 *Tgb.*, II, 226, # 2652, 14 Febr. 1843.
40 *Br.* II, 271, # 156, 17 June 1843.
41 *Tgb.*, II, 260, # 2752, 9 Aug. 1843.
42 *Tgb.*, II, 299, # 2864, 16 Nov. 1843.
43 *Br.*, II, 342, # 169, 5 Dec. 1843.
44 *Tgb.*, II, 338, # 2947, 19 Dec. 1843.
45 *Tgb.*, II, 395-396, # 3108, 28 April 1844.
46 *Tgb.*, II, 407, # 3144, 31 May 1844.
47 *Wke.*, VI, 361, 1844(?)
48 *Wke.*, VI, 360, 1844.
49 *Tgb.*, II, 423-424, # 3192, 1 Aug. 1844.
50 *Tgb.*, II, 441, # 3248, 18 Oct. 1844. Also *Wke.*, VI, 373, 1844(?), "Vergeblicher Wunsch."
51 *Tgb.*, III, 5, # 3290, 8 Jan. 1845. Cf., however, the verses from "Ein Spaziergang in Paris," of 28 May 1844, in *Wke.*, VI, 241: the artistic genius, such as Thorwaldsen, Raphael, Beethoven, Goethe is irreplaceable and, in fact, great artists grow ever more infrequent.
52 *Tgb.*, III, 44, # 3403, 21 Feb. 1845.
53 *Tgb.*, III, 91, # 3648, 30 June 1846.
54 *Tgb.*, III 112, # 3732, 3 Oct. 1846.
55 *Tgb.*, III, 114, # 3751.
56 *Tgb.*, I, 378, # 1691, 8 Oct. 1839.
57 *Tgb.*, I, 388, # 1727, 19 Oct. 1839, and *Tgb.*, II, 59, # 2095, 13 Aug. 1840.
58 *Tgb.*, II, 26-27, # 1958, 3 Apr. 1840.
59 *Tgb.*, II, 66, # 2129, 13 Sept. 1840.
60 *Tgb.*, II, 99, # 2290, 12 March 1841.
61 *Tgb.*, II, 155, # 2504, 2 March 1842.
62 *Tgb.*, I, 338, # 1515.
63 *Tgb.*, II, 46, # 2019, 1 May 1840.
64 *Tgb.*, II, 86, # 2220, 12 Jan. 1841.
65 *Tgb.*, II, 93, # 2253, 2 Feb. 1841.
66 *Tgb.*, II, 98, # 2280, 21 Feb. 1841.

67 *Tgb.*, II, 147, # 2463, 2 Feb. 1842.
68 *Tgb.*, II, 260, # 2752, 9 Aug. 1843.
69 *Br.*, II, 340-341, # 169, 5 Dec. 1843.
70 *Tgb.*, III, 161, # 3889.
71 *Tgb.*, III, 162, # 3892, 10 Jan. 1847.
72 *Tgb.*, III, 171-172, # 3914, 20 Jan. 1847.
73 *Br.*, IV, 94, # 263, 7 March 1848.
74 *Tgb.*, III, 298, # 4371, 15 March 1848.
75 *Tgb.*, III, 298, # 4372, 25 March 1848.
76 *Tgb.*, III, 299, # 4380, 28 March 1848.
77 *Tgb.*, III, 301, # 4390, 18 April 1848.
78 *Tgb.*, III, 302, # 4393, 18 Apr. 1848.
79 *Tgb.*, III, 304, # 4399, 20 May 1848.
80 *Tgb.*, III, 305, # 4403, ca. 20 May 1848.
81 *Br.*, IV, 124, # 276, 16 June 1848, to Gustav Kühne.
82 *Br.*, IV, 126-127, # 277, 14 August 1848 to Eduard Janinski.
83 *Tgb.*, III, 306, # 4411, 20 June 1848.
84 *Tgb.*, III, 318, # 4481, 31 Dec. 1848.
85 *Br.*, VIII, 26-27, # 917.
86 *Tgb.*, III, 350, # 4661, 1 Jan. 1850.
87 *Tgb.*, III, 369, # 4772, 29 Dec. 1850.
88 *Tgb.*, III, 382, # 4841, 1 March 1851.
89 *Tgb.*, III, 406, # 4938.
90 Cf. Meyer-Benfey, *Hebbels Agnes Bernauer* (Weimar, 1931) for an account of this play.
91 *Tgb.*, III, 413, # 4982, 24 Dec. 1851.
92 *Br.*, IV, 358-359, # 375, 16 Febr. 1852, to Karl Werner.
93 *Tgb.*, III, 422, # 5036, 31 Dec, 1851.
94 *Tgb.*, III, 423, # 5038, 7 Jan. 1852.
95 *Br.*, V, 34, # 409, 18 Aug. 1852, to Felix Bamberg.
96 *Br.*, VIII, 37-38, # 922, 9 Aug. 1852, to Saint René Taillandier.
97 *Br.*, V, 97, # 431, 10 Feb. 1853 to Adolf Pichler.
98 *Tgb.*, III, 430, # 5076, 18 Feb. 1853.
99 *Br.*, V, 106-107, # 437, 13 June 1853, to G. G. Gervinus.
100 *Br.*, V, 205, # 485, 14 Dec. 1854, to Friedrich Uechtritz.
101 *Br.*, V, 110, # 439, 24 June 1853.
102 *Tgb.*, IV, 91, # 5499, 21 Nov. 1856.
103 *Tgb.*, IV, 79, # 5448, 11 June 1856.
104 *Tgb.*, IV, 66, # 5438, 16 April 1856.
105 *Br.*, VI, 8, # 562, 12 March 1857.
106 *Br.*, VI, 74, # 582a, 10 Nov. 1857.
107 *Tgb.*, IV, 113, # 5583, 7 Apr. 1857.
108 *Tgb.*, IV, 8, # 5891, 31 March 1861; and *Tgb.*, IV, 355, # 6328, 12 April 1863.
109 *Tgb.*, IV, 112, # 5578, 20 March 1857.
110 *Tgb.*, IV, 355-356, # 6334, 17 June(?) 1863.
111 *Tgb.*, IV, 131, # 5660, 25 March 1859.
112 *Br.*, VII, 151-152, # 770, 3 March 1862, to Adolph Strodtmann.

113 *Br.*, VII, 266, # 828, 25 Oct. 1862, to Friedrich Uechtritz.
114 *Br.*, VI, 266-267, # 656, 25 July 1859, to Friedrich Uechtritz.
115 *Tgb.*, IV, 230, # 5992, 26 Nov. 1862.
116 *Tgb.*, IV, 203, # 5937, 6 Nov. 1861.
117 *Br.*, VII, 291, # 841, 27 Jan. 1863, to Sigmund Engländer.
118 *Tgb.*, IV, 277, # 6102, 8 March 1863.

PART TWO

1 The following discussion of Hebbel's theories draws heavily upon the essays *Mein Wort über das Drama* (31 July 1843) and *Vorwort zu Maria Magdalene* (March 1844), which are the major sources for Hebbel's theory of drama and metaphysics, though, as von Wiese points out (*Die deutsche Tragödie von Lessing bis Hebbel*, II, 353-376 passim), the Hegelian terminology of these essays is apt to give the impression of an optimistic and dialectic conception of history, which must be corrected by a more careful and empathic reading of the diaries and poems, as well as the plays. It should also be recognized that, as has been pointed out by Oskar Walzel, T. M. Campbell, and others, Hebbel later repudiated metaphysical speculation, but did retain his belief in the conflict of the individual and the Idea as the basis of tragedy.
2 *Wke.*, XI, 56.
3 *Tgb.*, II, 66, # 2129, 13 Sept. 1840.
4 *Wke.*, XI, 45-46.
5 *Wke.*, XI, 3-4.
6 *Wke.*, XI, 45-46.
7 *Ibid.*
8 *Tgb.*, II, 95, # 2262, 2 Febr. 1841.
9 *Wke.*, XI, 30.
10 *Tgb.*, II, 174, # 2531, 18 April 1842. Cf. also the poem *"Die Freiheit der Sünde," Wke.*, VI, 312, 4 Oct. 1845, in which the same basic idea is given the additional variation that the attempt to hold one's breath will lead only to death without making any change in the atmosphere.
11 *Tgb.*, I, 337-338, # 1510, 24 Febr. 1837.
12 *Wke.*, XI, 31.
13 *Wke.*, XI, 32-33.
14 *Wke.*, XI, 27.
15 *Wke.*, XI, 40-41.
16 *Wke.*, XI, 43.
17 *Tgb.*, III, 269-270, # 4274, 18 Sept. 1847. This is the tragic process which Hebbel has represented in *Agnes Bernauer* and in *Gyges und sein Ring*.
18 *Tgb.*, II, 388, # 3086, 25 March 1844. Cf. also the sonnet "Welt und Ich," *Wke.*, VI, 317-318, spring 1842.
19 *Judith*, begun 2 Oct. 1839, completed 27 Jan. 1840.

20 *Tgb.*, II, 26-27, # 1958, 3 April 1840.
21 *Tgb.*, II, 26, # 1958, 3 April 1840.
22 *Genoveva*, begun 13 Sept. 1840, completed 1 March 1841. Cf. *Tgb.*, II, 102, # 2304, 13 March 1841, where Hebbel writes that *Judith* bears the same relation to *Genoveva* as the negative pole to the positive.
23 *Tgb.*, I, 322-323, # 1475, 2 Febr. 1839.
24 *Nachspiel zur Genoveva*, completed 21 Jan. 1851.
25 For the term cf. K. Ziegler, *Mensch und Welt in der Tragödie Hebbels* (Berlin, 1938).
26 Ll. 508-511.
27 Ll. 470-471.
28 Ll. 785-786.
29 Ll. 1446-1451.
30 *Tgb.*, II, 99, # 2290, 12 March 1841.
31 *Tgb.*, I, 319-321, # 1475, 2 Febr. 1839.
32 Ll. 1552-1555.
33 *Tgb.*, I, 321, # 1475, 2 Febr. 1839.
34 *Tgb.*, I, 322, # 1475, 2 Febr. 1839.
35 Ll. 722-724.
36 *Tgb.*, II, 111, # 2337, 29 May 1841.
37 *Tgb.*, I, 322, # 1475, 2 Febr. 1839.
38 Cf. *Tgb.*, II, 112, # 2342, 30 May 1841; 147, # 2464, 10 Febr. 1842; 150, # 2472, 14 Febr. 1842.
39 Cf. Paul G. Graham, *The Relation of History to Drama in the Works of Friedrich Hebbel* (Smith College Studies in Modern Languages, XV, Nos. 1-2, October 1933-January 1934), p. 26.
40 Ll. 2880-2897.
41 *Tgb.*, II, 146, # 2460, 31 Jan. 1842.
42 The supposition that this entry is to be taken rather seriously is given some support by the consideration that in the play Siegfried, on his way home to the Palatinate, is detained by illness in the intermediate city of Strassburg.
43 Begun in February 1838; completed 29 November 1841.
44 Begun 10 March 1843, completed 4 December 1843.
45 Cf. *Tgb.*, II, 324-325, # 2910, 4 Dec. 1843.
46 *Br.*, II, 348, # 171.
47 For a discussion of the lower middle class attitude toward pre-marital relations of betrothed couples see Werner's introduction to the play, *Wke.*, II, xviii-xix.
48 Act III, vii, 62.
49 Act I, v, 28-29.
50 Act II, i, 40.
51 Act II, v, 41.
52 Act II, v, 51.
53 Act I, iv, 18-19.
54 Act II, vi, 52.
55 Act III, viii, 63.
56 Act I, iii, 15; v, 23-24; vii, 34.

57 Begun November 1845, completed 23 October 1847.
58 *Tgb.*, III, 187, # 3943, 30 Jan. 1847.
59 *Tgb.*, III, 187, # 3943, 30 Jan. 1847.
60 Begun 12 September 1846, completed 9 January 1847.
61 *Tgb.*, III, 187, # 3943, 30 Jan. 1847.
62 *Wke.*, II, 379-380.
62a Cf. *Tgb.*, II, 239, # 2664, 6 March 1843; 295, # 2845, 11 Nov. 1843; 269, # 2776, 29 Aug. 1843.
63 Begun 23 February 1847, completed 14 November 1848.
64 *Tgb.*, II 328-329, # 2926, 8 Dec. 1843.
65 *Br.*, IV, 129, # 277, 14 Aug. 1848.
66 *Br.*, IV, 74, # 256, 22 Dec. 1847.
67 *Wke.*, XI, 253, Hebbel's review of Massenger's *Ludovico*.
68 Ll. 801-819.
69 Ll. 148-156, 775-783.
70 Ll. 2283-2325.
71 Ll. 2775-2790.
72 Ll. 79-95.
73 Ll. 836-843.
74 Ll. 1012-1039.
75 Cf. Benno von Wiese, *Die deutsche Tragödie von Lessing bis Hebbel*, (Hamburg, 1948), II, 418ff.
76 Ll. 1830-1832.
77 L. 1901.
78 Ll. 1906-1910.
79 *Loc. cit.* and ll. 1803-1807.
80 Ll. 1646-1647.
81 Ll. 1778-1780.
82 Ll. 1833-1845.
83 Ll. 2187-2194.
84 Ll. 2201-2205.
85 Can one individual *sin* against another? Hebbel says no. The principle which can be sinned against is something which transcends individuals as such. Not even the worst sophist, he says, will dare to identify with an individual the principle which can be sinned against by another individual and then deny that, these individuals, being considered as members of a cosmic moral order, as monads in which the highest Idea seeks mysteriously to manifest itself, are justified in proportion to their power. Cf. *Wke.*, XI, 27.
86 Cf. H. T. Rötscher's introductory remarks in *Jahrbücher für dramatsche Kunst und Literatur* (1849) as quoted in Werner's edition of Hebbel *Wke.*, II, 414-415. Werner quite correctly observes that Rötscher must have based his remarks on letters from Hebbel, of whose style and language the passage is so reminiscent.
87 Ll. 3037-3042.
88 Cf. *Br.*, VI, 55-56, # 412, 15 Sept. 1852, to Arnold Runge.
89 Begun 1 April 1849, completed 19 May 1849.
90 *Tgb.*, I, 82, # 442, October or November 1836.

NOTES

91 Ll. 1033-1057.
92 Ll. 1305-1318.
93 Composition begun 1845, first act completed 12 June 1849, second act completed 25 October 1850.
94 Cf. *Br.*, VIII, 45-46, # 922, 9 August 1852, to Saint René Taillandier.
95 Cf. *Tgb.*, III, 185, # 3943, 30 Jan. 1847.
96 Begun 22 Sept. 1851, completed 24 Dec. 1851.
97 Cf. Act IV, iv, 202, ll. 12-14; Act V, iv, 219, ll. 11-12.
98 *Tgb.*, III, 413, # 4982, 24 Dec. 1851.
99 *Br.*, IV, 350, # 322, 26 Jan. 1852.
100 *Br.*, V, 205, # 485, 14 Dec. 1854.
101 *Tgb.*, III, 406, # 4941, 30 Sept. 1851.
102 *Tgb.*, III, 2-3, # 3286, January 1845.
103 *Br.*, VII, 291, # 841, 27 Jan. 1863.
104 *Hebbels Agnes Bernauer* (Weimar 1931).
105 *Ibid.*, pp. 30, 72.
106 *Die deutsche Tragödie von Lessing bis Hebbel*, II, 430ff.
107 "Die Doppelstellung Herzog Albrechts in Hebbels *Agnes Bernauer*," *MFDU*, XXXI, 209ff.
108 Act II, xvii, 154.
109 *Tgb.*, III, 384, # 4848, 11 March 1851: "Auch das Weltgericht hat Pausen."
110 Act IV, iv, 202.
111 Act IV, iii, 200.
112 Act V, vi, 224.
113 *Br.*, V, 97, # 431, 10 Febr. 1853, to Adolf Pichler.
114 Act V, vi, 225.
115 Act V, x, 233.
116 Begun Dec. 1853, completed 14 November 1854.
117 *Br.*, VI, 74, # 582a, 10 Nov. 1857, to Georg Cotta.
118 *Br.*, V, 203-204, # 485, 14 Dec. 1854.
119 Cf. the introductory distichs to the effect that the mythical apparatus is intended to give an atmosphere to the play, not to symbolize fate, which comes only from the human breast; also a letter to Sigmund Engländer (*Br.*, VII, 304, # 847, 23 Febr. 1863) in which he repeats the belief that the ring is not essential to the play.
120 *Br.*, V, 203-204, # 485, 14 Dec. 1854, to Friedrich Uechtritz.
121 *Br.*, V, 306, # 535, 16 May 1856, to Karl Werner.
122 *Br.*, V, 204, # 485, 14 Dec. 1854, to Friedrich Uechtritz.
123 Ll. 962-964.
124 Ll. 329-341.
125 Ll. 1205-1206.
126 L. 991.
127 Ll. 1224-1228.
128 Ll. 1268-1273.
129 Ll. 987-993.
130 Ll. 347-349.
131 Ll. 906-941, esp. 936-941.

132 Ll. 942-945.
133 Ll. 1205-1206.
134 Ll. 1517-1518.
135 L. 1572.
136 Ll. 1584-1586.
137 Ll. 1963-1964.
138 Ll. 1947-1953.
139 Cf. p. 28, above.
140 Ll. 1801-1802, 1822-1825.
141 Ll. 1848-1850.
142 Ll. 13-15.
143 Ll. 76-80.
144 Ll. 61-69.
145 L. 282.
146 Ll. 991-993.
147 Ll. 431-440.
148 Ll. 1074-1078.
149 Cf. p. 55 above, also Pio Eggstein, *Friedrich Hebbels Drama Gyges und sein Ring* (Dissertation, University of Zürich, 1948), pp. 11-12, who points out that the play must not be viewed exclusively from the historical perspective.
150 Ll. 1718-1722.
151 Ll. 448-449.
152 Ll. 1928-1932.
153 Ll. 358-397 and 554-561.
154 Ll. 1849-1850.
155 Cf. *Tgb.*, III, 55, # 3475, 3 July 1845: "Man and woman in their undisguised relation to one another: the former destroyed by the latter." Cf. also Elise Dosenheimer, *Das zentrale Problem in der Tragödie Hebbels* (Halle, 1925).
156 Ll. 1778-1800.
157 Ll. 1809-1812.
158 Ll. 1806-1807.
159 Ll. 1827-1830.
160 Ll. 1443-1445.
161 Ll. 48 and 86.
162 Ll. 258-273.
163 Ll. 534-537.
164 Ll. 622-624.
165 Ll. 660-667.
166 L. 458.
167 L. 561.
168 Ll. 1925-1927.
169 L. 1361.
170 Ll. 501-510.
171 Ll. 1418-1424.
172 Ll. 1492-1494.
173 Begun Oct. 1855, completed 22 March 1860.

174 *Br.*, VI, 193, # 626, 24 Aug. 1858.
175 *Br.*, VII, 12, # 702, 21 Jan. 1861.
176 Cf. *Wke.*, IV, "Lesarten und Anmerkungen," 369-373.
177 Ll. 1062-1069.
178 Ll. 2689-2691.
179 Ll. 100-105.
180 Ll. 2689-2691.
181 Ll. 4479-4490.
182 Ll. 171-179, 568.
183 Ll. 537-650.
184 Ll. 642-650.
185 Ll. 1735-1736, 1737, 1905-1907.
186 Ll. 1752-1754, 1765-1768.
187 Ll. 3915-3975.
188 Begun Dec. 1857, composition continued until the end of Hebbel's life.
189 *Br.*, VI, 244, # 646, 24 March 1859.
190 *Tgb.*, I, 228, # 1047.
191 *Tgb.*, II, 88, # 2231.
192 *Tgb.*, III, 333-334, # 4566.
193 Oskar Walzel in his book *Friedrich Hebbel und seine Dramen* (Leipzig, Berlin, 1927), pp. 134-137, quite rightly insists that the play is a fragment, but he would seem to be pushing caution a bit too far by insisting that such a relatively complete fragment and one which, especially in the masterly third and fourth acts, particularly the "revelation" scenes eight, nine, and ten of the fourth act, shows no slackening of Hebbel's creative force, perhaps even the contrary, does not reveal enough of the writer's intention to be significant. Walzel finds it hard to accept *Demetrius* because it is so different from all the preceding plays as Walzel interprets them. It is quite true, Walzel's "Wendepunkt" theory is inadequate to account for *Demetrius*. A pertinent question is: Should not, in view of this fact, the theory be reexamined in its application to the earlier plays, notably *Genoveva, Agnes Bernauer,* and *Gyges und sein Ring,* and, if found inadequate there, too, as it seems to be, discarded?
194 Cf., for example, *Br.*, VI, 207, 216, 224-226.
195 Hebbel's spelling of the names will be retained, although they are in many instances arbitrary and incorrect.
196 L. 385.
197 L. 593.
198 Ll. 1695-1698.
199 Ll. 1275-1295.
200 Ll. 414-419.
201 Ll. 755-784.
202 Ll. 1575-1608.
203 Ll. 3024-3026.
204 Ll. 930-937.
205 Ll. 920-929.
206 Ll. 944-950.

207 Ll. 930-1004.
208 Ll. 962-972.
209 Ll. 2220-2224. But see Benno von Wiese, *Die deutsche Tragödie von Lessing bis Hebbel*, II, 458.
210 Ll. 3055-3074.

PART THREE

1 *Tgb.*, I, 294, # 1364, 28 Nov. 1838.
2 *Tgb.*, IV, 277, # 6102, 8 March 1863.
3 *Tgb.*, I, 338, # 1515, 24 Febr. 1839.
4 *Tgb.*, I, 306, # 1418, 6 Jan. 1839.
5 *Tgb.*, II, 407, # 3144, 31 May 1844.
6 *Tgb.*, III, 44, # 3403, 21 Febr. 1845.
7 *Tgb.*, IV, 112, # 5578, 20 March 1857.
8 *Tgb.*, II, 79, # 2197, 2 Dec. 1840.
9 *Tgb.*, I, 348, # 1546, 8 April 1839.
10 *Tgb.*, II, 26, # 1958, 3 April 1840.
11 *Tgb.*, III, 54, # 3466, 20 April 1845.
12 *Tgb.*, IV, 232, # 6001, 26 Nov. 1862.
13 *Tgb.*, II, 110, # 2329, 29 April 1841.
14 *Tgb.*, II, 5, # 1883, 3 Jan. 1840.
15 *Tgb.*, II, 270, # 2784, 20 Sept. 1843.
16 *Tgb.*, I, 18, # 77.
17 *Tgb.*, II, 174, # 2531, 18 April 1842.
18 *Tgb.*, II, 265, # 2759, 19 Aug. 1843.
19 *Tgb.*, II, 256, # 2731, 12 July 1843.
20 *Tgb.*, II, 239, # 2663, 6 March 1843.
21 *Tgb.*, III, 210, # 4019a, 10 March 1847.
22 *Wke.*, VI, 376.
23 *Tgb.*, III, 112, # 3736, 3 Oct. 1846.
24 *Tgb.*, I, 391, # 1744, 28 Oct. 1839.
25 *Tgb.*, I, 377, # 1687, 8 Oct. 1839.
26 *Tgb.*, II, 377, # 3028, 31 Jan. 1844.
27 *Tgb.*, II, 100, # 2302, 12 March 1841.
28 *Tgb.*, II, 33, # 1971, 6 April 1840.
29 *Tgb.*, II, 67, # 2137, 25 Sept. 1840.
30 *Tgb.*, III, 112, # 3739, 3 Oct. 1846.
31 *Tgb.*, II, 117, # 2359, 1 July 1841.
32 *Tgb.*, IV, 77, # 5847, 21 Jan. 1861.
33 Wolfgang Liepe in his article, "Der Schlüssel zum Weltbild Hebbels: Gotthilf Heinrich Schubert," *MFDU*, XLIII (March 1951), writes that he feels he has discovered the all-important source of Hebbel's view of life in the writings of Gotthilf Heinrich Schubert. His very interesting essay points out curious parallels that are very suggestive, indeed. Presumably, he will in a more comprehensive and pre-

cise study give definite and documented proof that Hebbel had read the works in question. As Professor Liepe himself maintains, the significance of his thesis is not to demonstrate that Hebbel "lifted" his basic philosophy from any specific sources, but to illuminate the growth-process of his mind. If positive proof of this is established, it will surely be very illuminating for the force with which Hebbel experienced things and which, apparently, allowed him to assimilate another's thoughts and feelings with the same intensity as he assimilated his own life-experiences.

It must be pointed out, however, that in precisely the most important point of comparison Hebbel and Schubert take exactly opposite positions. As we have seen, in Hebbel's view the individual forms are indispensable to the Absolute, which, but for them must terminate in static rigidity. As Liepe points out (pp. 121, 123, and passim), in Schubert's view the vital flow of original nature has been transformed into a static co-existence of individual stereotypic forms. Hebbel's view surely contradicts Schubert's: can it be dependent upon it?

34 *Tgb.*, I, 90, # 501, 15 Dec. 1836.
35 *Tgb.*, I, 87, # 476, 10 Dec. 1836.
36 *Tgb.*, III, 245, # 4214, 20 June 1847.
37 *Tgb.*, II, 95, # 2262, 2 Febr. 1841.
38 *Tgb.*, II, 138, # 2440, 14 Jan., 1842.
39 *Tgb.*, IV, 112, # 5578, 20 March 1857.
40 *Tgb.*, IV, 131, # 5659, 25 March 1859.
41 *Tgb.*, II, 286, # 2823, 6 Nov. 1843.
42 *Tgb.*, II, 373, # 3012, 27 Jan. 1844.
43 *Tgb.*, III, 44, # 3401, 21 Febr. 1845.
44 *Tgb.*, I, 6, # 14-16, 1 April 1835.
45 *Tgb.*, III, # 3317, 16 Febr. 1845.
46 Cf. the following diary entries: # 32, 33, 2596, 4453, 4837, 4850, 5166, 5583, 5662.
47 *Tgb.*, II, 192, # 2576, 29 July 1842.
48 *Tgb.*, II, 326, # 2920, 6 Dec. 1843.
49 *Tgb.*, II, 178, # 2550, 13 May 1842.
50 *Tgb.*, IV, 135, # 5688, 1 April 1859.
51 Cf. Wilhelm Waetzoldt, *Hebbel und die Philosophie seiner Zeit* (Berlin, 1903); Ludwig Marcuse, "Der Hegelianer Friedrich Hebbel gegen Hegel," *MFDU*, XXIX, pp. 506-514; also H. M. Wolff, "Noch einmal Hebbel und Hegel," *MFDU*, XL, pp. 157-159; and Wolfgang Liepe, "Der Schlüssel zum Weltbild Hebbels: Gotthilf Heinrich Schubert," *MFDU*, XLIII, pp. 117-132.
52 *Tgb.*, I, 171, # 773.
53 *Tgb.*, II, 101, # 2303, 12 March 1841.
54 *Tgb.*, II, 57, # 2078, 13 August 1840.
55 "Das abgeschiedene Kind an seine Mutter," *Wke.*, VI, 294, 17 Dec. 1843.
56 *Wke.*, VI, 149, 15 August 1840.
57 "Erleuchtung," *Wke.*, VI, 255, 1836.

58 "Mysterium," *Wke.*, VI, 322, spring 1842.
59 "Dem Schmerz sein Recht," *Wke.*, VI, 293, 21 Sept. 1841.
60 "Reminiszenz," *Wke.*, VI, 258, 29 Jan. 1843.
61 *Wke.*, VI, 255, 22 March 1835.
62 *Wke.*, VI, 227, 31 May 1836.
63 *Wke.*, VII, 51, 28 July 1831.
64 *Wke.*, VI, 179, 4 April 1841.
65 "Vater und Sohn," *Wke.*, VII, 152, 31.Oct.1837.
66 "Vater Unser," *Wke.*, VI, 169, 5 Dec. 1839.
67 "Vater und Sohn," (sic), *Wke.*, VI, 427, Oct. 1862.
68 *Tgb.*, I, 279-280, # 1323, Nov., 1838.
69 *Wke.*, VI, 258, 2 Febr. 1843.
70 *Wke.*, VI, 263, 24 Febr. 1837.
71 "Wüstenbild," *Wke.*, VI, 328, 1851.
72 "Sturmabend," *Wke.*, VI, 143, 19 May 1841.
73 *Wke.*, VI, 143, 6 May 1836.
74 Cf. T. M. Campbell, *The Life and Works of Friedrich Hebbel* (Boston, 1919), p. 110.

BIBLIOGRAPHY

The following list of books is not intended to be an exhaustive compilation of Hebbel-literature.

Bartels, Adolf. *C. F. Hebbel.* Leipzig, 1899.
Blaustein, Leopold. *Das Gotteserlebnis in Hebbels Dramen.* Berlin, 1929.
Bohrig, K. *Die Probleme der Hebbelschen Tragödie.* Rathenow, 1899.
Brun, Louis. *Hebbel. Mit besonderer Berücksichtigung seiner Persönlichkeit und seiner Lyrik.* Leipzig, 1922.
Campbell, T. M. "Hebbel's *Herodes und Mariamne* ll. 1289-1295," *MLN*, XLIV, 250-253.
id. "History as Costume in Hebbel's Drama." *MLN*, XLI, 489-495.
id. *The Life and Works of Friedrich Hebbel.* Boston, 1919.
Dosenheimer, Elise. *Das zentrale Problem in der Tragödie Friedrich Hebbels.* Halle, 1925.
Georgy, E. A. *Die Tragödie Hebbels nach ihrem Ideengehalt.* Leipzig, 1911.
Graham, P. G. *The Relation of History to Drama in the Works of Friedrich Hebbel.* Smith College Studies in Modern Languages, XV, Nos. 1-2, 1933-1934.
id. "The Principle of Necessity in Hebbel's Theory of Tragedy," *GR*, XV, 258-262.
Henel, Heinrich. "Realismus und Tragik in Hebbels Dramen," *PMLA*, LIII, 502-518.
Hewett-Thayer, H. W. "Ludwig Tieck and Hebbel's Tragedy of Beauty," *GR*, XI, 16-25.

Ittner, R. T. "Comments on Hebbel's Use of Dreams," *GQ*, XV, 193-199.
Jokisch, W. "Hebbel-Literatur, 1919-1930," *Archiv*, 163, 34ff.
Krumm, J. *Die Tragödie Hebbels, ihre Stellung und Bedeutung in der Entwicklung des Dramas*. Hebbel-Forschungen, III, Berlin.
Kuh, Emil. *Hebbel*. Wien, 1877. Third ed., 1912.
Lang, Renée. "Le Roi Candaule (Gide) and Gyges' Ring," *PMLA*, LXIII.
Liepe, Wolfgang. "Existenzschuld und persönliche Schuld im Drama Hebbels," *PMLA*, LXIV.
id. "Der Schlüssel zum Weltbild Hebbels: Gotthilf Heinrich Schubert," *MFDU*, XLIII, 117-132.
Lukács, Georg von. "Zur Soziologie des modernen Dramas," *Archiv für Sozialwissenschaft und Politik*, XXXVIII.
Lyle, C. C. "Hebbel's *Herodes und Mariamne* and *Agnes Bernauer*: Contrast or Continuity of Theme?" *PMLA*, LXIV.
Marcuse, Ludwig. "Der Hegelianer Friedrich Hebbel—gegen Hegel," *MFDU*, XXXIX, 506-514.
Meyer-Benfey, H. *Judith*. Göttingen, 1913.
id. *Hebbels Agnes Bernauer*. Weimar, 1931.
Pargeter, H. Joan. "The Relations between Men and Women in Hebbel's Plays," *PMLA*, LXIV.
Pfeiffer, F. L. "The Moral Problem in Hebbel's Drama," *GR*, II.
Poppe, Theodor. "Hebbel und sein Drama," *Palaestra*, VIII.
Porterfield, A. W. "Friedrich Hebbel's Use of Jewels," *PMLA*, XXX.
Schapire-Neurath, Anna. *Friedrich Hebbel*. Leipzig, 1909.
Scheunert, A. *Der Pantragismus als System der Weltanschauung und Aesthetik Hebbels*. Second ed.; Leipzig, 1930.
Schreiber, S. E. "Bourgeois Ideals in Weisse, Lessing, Hebbel, and Wedekind," *PMLA*, LXIV.
Schueler, H. "Hebbel's Poetic Use of the Dream," *GQ*, XIV, 1-17.
Shepard, F. L. "Hebbel's Gedankenkasten in the *Maria Magdalene*," *JEGP*, XXX.
Sommerfeld, Martin. *Hebbel und Goethe*. Bonn, 1923.
Staley, Ruth. *Hebbel as a Critic of 19th Century German Literature*, University of Wisconsin Summaries of Doctoral Dissertations, III.
Waetzoldt, Wilhelm. *Hebbel und die Philosophie seiner Zeit*. Dissertation, Berlin, 1903.
Wagner, A. W. *Hebbels Drama, eine Stilbetrachtung des Dichters und seiner Kunst*. Hamburg, 1911.
Walzel, O. *Hebbelprobleme*. Leipzig, 1909.
id. *Hebbel und seine Dramen*. Leipzig, Berlin, 1927.
id. "Vom Wesen des Tragischen," *Euphorion*, XXXIV.
Werner, R. M. *Hebbel. Ein Lebensbild*. Berlin, 1913.
Winterfeld, Achim von. *Friedrich Hebbel: Sein Leben und seine Werke*. Dresden, 1908.
Wolff, Hans M. "Die Doppelstellung Herzog Albrechts in Hebbels *Agnes Bernauer*," *MFDU*, XXXI.
id. "Noch einmal Hebbel und Hegel," *MFDU*, XL.

Wright, James D. *Hebbel's Theory of Tragic Guilt and its Application in Judith and Agnes Bernauer.* University of Wisconsin Summaries of Doctoral Dissertations, VII.
Wütschke, H. *Hebbel-Bibliographie.* Berlin, 1910.
Zagel, Milton. "The Family Problem in the Dramas of Hebbel," *PMLA*, LXIII.
Zieglschmid, A. J. F. *"Beiträge zu Friedrich Hebbels Charakterkunde. Ein psychologischer Deutungsversuch.* Hebbel-Forschungen, XXII, Berlin.
Zinkernagel, F. *Die Grundlagen der Hebbelschen Tragödie.* Berlin, 1904.

www.ingramcontent.com/pod-product-compliance
Lightning Source LLC
Chambersburg PA
CBHW031321150426
43191CB00005B/280